FOUNDATIONS OF ENGLISH ADMINISTRATIVE LAW

A PUBLICATION OF THE AMES FOUNDATION

The Ames Foundation was founded in 1910 by contributions of the friends of James Barr Ames for the purpose of continuing the advancement of legal knowledge and aiding the improvement of the law.

FOUNDATIONS

OF ENGLISH ADMINISTRATIVE LAW

Certiorari and Mandamus in the Seventeenth Century

EDITH G. HENDERSON

HARVARD UNIVERSITY PRESS

Cambridge, Massachusetts · 1963

Distributed in Great Britain by Oxford University Press, London

Library of Congress Catalog Card Number 63-11421
Printed in the United States of America

PREFACE

In this study of the early roots of modern administrative law I have been encouraged and aided by the Harvard Law School—for although the school rightly considers its chief function to be the training of practicing lawyers, it has always taught law "in the grand manner" and has encouraged and sought out scholars to take advantage of its magnificent historical collections. I particularly wish to thank Professor Louis L. Jaffe, who suggested the problem, stood by me in the first difficult stages of learning my way into legal-historical materials, and helped me greatly to clarify my thinking; and Professors Mark Howe and Samuel E. Thorne. Thanks are also due to the United States Educational Commission for a Fulbright grant in 1955-56 which enabled me to do research in the Public Record Office; and to the Harvard Law School Library which as my employer in recent years has been more than tolerant of the time required for research and writing on this scale.

The materials upon which this study is based are both historical and legal. It is hoped that it will interest both lawyers who wish to know more about the early development of their profession—a profession which in common-law countries can look back on more than seven hundred years of unbroken development—and historians who realize the importance of the legal framework within which a society operates at any given period.

E. G. H.

CONTENTS

FOUNDATIONS OF ENGLISH ADMINISTRATIVE LAW

Passages in law French have been translated, almost word for word. Peculiarities of seventeenth-century spelling and capitalization have not been preserved in these translations.

INTRODUCTION

THIS BOOK, a study in the beginnings of Anglo-American administrative law, focuses mainly on one aspect of the relationship of English subjects to their government during the seventeenth and early eighteenth centuries. Supposing that an Englishman felt himself hurt by the illegal action of a government official, what could he do? Could he challenge the official action in court with a view to stopping it or obtaining redress for his wrong? Could this be done promptly and easily?

In the years 1600-1750, roughly, two new legal remedies—new modes of proceeding in the courts—were developed which gave the aggrieved subject quicker and easier relief from illegal action by officials. It may reasonably be said that these two new remedies, certiorari "to quash" and mandamus, made possible the whole complex structure of modern administrative law. In the broader fields of the common law, property, contracts, torts, as a great pioneer pointed out, "substantive law has at first the look of being gradually secreted in the interstices of procedure."[1] In the same manner the key modern doctrine for review of government action by the courts—that the review should be limited in scope and so leave room for administrative

[1] Sir Henry Maine, *Early Law and Custom* (London, 1883), p. 389. Cf. F. W. Maitland, *The Forms of Action at Common Law* (Cambridge, 1936).

discretion—arose in connection with these two seventeenth century modes of procedure.

One of the most fascinating aspects of these two new remedies is their steady, continuous growth through some of the most turbulent years of English history. Between 1640 and 1689 England underwent a bloody civil war, revolutionary constitutional changes, a restoration and a second bloodless revolution. The relationship of King and Parliament was so fundamentally changed that 1649 may be treated as the end of medieval England or 1660 as the beginning of modern times. Yet in the law courts the slow growth of these and other legal doctrines continued from case to case without sharp breaks, with scarcely even a change of pace.

As part of the intellectual development of the years 1600-1750 the uses of dissent began to be understood. Gradually a distinction seems to have been made between sedition or contempt for authority and legitimate disagreement, and with this distinction came a need for remedies to protect the dissenter. More prosaically, the average substantial citizen of this time was beginning to feel the impact of broader economic activity by local government, and to find that its procedures were becoming more summary. Certain of its organs, particularly the justices of peace and the sewers commissions, were being given functions that called for the use of rather broad discretion.

The traditional procedures used by these local bodies, being criminal or quasi-criminal in their conception, were ill-adapted to carrying out these new programs. Moreover the traditional procedures had afforded only rather rudimentary methods for the aggrieved citizen to test the legality of the officials' activities. With the increasing number of programs of poor relief, drainage of marshes, and the like, it became clear that existing remedies against officials were inadequate, and the citizen demanded new remedies.

In this demand for new remedies one of the great paradoxes of organized society was making itself felt: the necessity of general rules of law which are laid down in advance to be followed by citizen and government alike; and at the same time, the necessity of specialized knowledge, flexibility, and creativeness in the administration of government, a condition which requires that officials be given wide discretion in some things. The key to this paradox is the doctrine of judicial review with limited scope. It is our good fortune that in a general way this doctrine was worked out in England at a relatively early date, to control the relations between local government and central government. Thus it lay ready at hand when the problems of the Industrial Revolution cried out for government action.

There are three aspects of the doctrine of limited judicial review as it exists in Anglo-American law. The first is obvious: there must be general standards of conduct and purpose for government agencies and officials as well as for private citizens. These standards are formulated by a legislature which in modern times has usually been an elected assembly, more or less representative in character. Such a body is not a prerequisite for the "rule of law" but it is necessary that the government should act by means of general rules and not by the whim or convenience of the moment.

Second, it must be possible for the individual citizen whose activity or property is affected by government action to test whether government officials have applied those general standards properly. In our society a court of general jurisdiction is the testing place, so that broadly speaking the same criteria of legality are applied to public and private controversies, and to citizen and official alike. This is perhaps not strictly necessary; possibly a specialized constitutional court or some other institutional setting would do as well. But it is essential that the judge in such cases should be independent of the day-to-day exigencies of administration.

Third, some kinds of decision must be left to the final determination of the administrative officials. When a modern government undertakes a complex program of social service or economic regulation, neither lawmaker nor courts can be expected to make all the decisions. Neither lawmaker nor courts with their generalized responsibility can know all the details of railroad administration, atomic power, education, agriculture, and thousands of other activities on which the law may impinge in modern society. No lawmaker can foresee all possible future developments, so as to lay down rules for them in advance. No representative legislature, subject to pressures from a multitude of interest groups legitimate and not so legitimate, can achieve complete agreement even for all the cases that can be foreseen. Some questions will and should always be left open, to be answered only when they arise; that is, in modern society there is and must always be room for administrative discretion.

In such complex areas of government activity it is now common for the legislature to set up a specialized agency whose members can acquire expert knowledge of a field or set of problems—the Interstate Commerce Commission for railroads, Industrial Accident Board for workmen's compensation, and the like. Such an agency's decisions can almost always be reviewed by the courts to test whether they conform to the broad standards set by the statute; but the courts will refrain from deciding every detail of fact and even some details of law out of respect for the agency's specialized knowledge of its particular field.

This threefold division of labor, between a legislator, an administrative official, and an independent judge, is a necessary condition for the rule of law in modern society and therefore for democratic government itself. General standards of law do not in themselves guarantee freedom, for the legislator may be an absolute monarch and the laws repressive. But without general laws, freedom is impossible in any society larger than the Garden of Eden. (For that matter, who would say that there was no difference between Bismarck's Prussian *Rechtsstaat* and Hitler's nearly absolute tyranny?) But general standards of law and decisions democratically made will be little more than pious words unless their application by administrative officials can be tested before judges independent of those officials.

The doctrine of limited judicial review was worked out in England during the seventeenth and early eighteenth centuries, in connection with the agencies of local government. Partly implicit in the older remedy of prohibition and in common-law damage suits, it was made explicit in the new remedies of certiorari and mandamus. In the eighteenth century the doctrine was a part of the great compromise by which the Tory gentlemen of England did as they saw fit in the country while the Whigs controlled the central government. In later times, when the English and American social conscience began to catch up with technical organization, it provided a means of regulating industrial life.

The doctrine of judicial review as worked out in the seventeenth and eighteenth centuries was less happy in its details than in the notion as a whole. Theoretical emphasis at that time was on "jurisdiction," an elusive concept of the agency's or justices' "power" to hear the question at all or to take a given action. Questions that had been labeled as "jurisdictional" could be reviewed as of right. But questions that had not been so labeled could be reviewed by the central courts only if the agency in effect consented to review, by stating reasons for the action that had been challenged. Thus according to the classical theory of the eighteenth century and later, a man might be aggrieved by official action that was clearly illegal, but be unable to challenge it in the courts because the issue was not considered "jurisdictional." But in fact much less injustice of this kind resulted than might have been expected. One reason for this was that, when a case of obvious injustice and illegality came before the courts, some formula of words could usually (though not always) be found to call the issue "jurisdictional":

Neither in magisterial law nor in administrative law have the superior courts applied a consistent theory of jurisdiction. In general they have refused to accept the doctrine that, whenever an inferior tribunal has jurisdiction to inquire into a matter for the purpose of giving a decision, its findings thereon, whether they be right or wrong, are conclusive; but it cannot be said that they have ever definitively rejected this doctrine . . . There is no want of modern authority to draw upon when a court is inclined to hold that an erroneous finding by a statutory tribunal goes to jurisdiction. But although the courts are usually prepared to set aside decisions which in their opinion are wrong, and to justify their intervention on jurisdictional grounds, it would be incorrect to say that the scope of jurisdictional control is exactly coextensive with the powers of review that a court thinks it desirable to exercise in any particular case.[2]

This confused state of affairs arose because in the seventeenth century, in the early days of judicial review, the courts inclined to the view that every question of statutory construction was jurisdictional, quite aside from the meaning of the word in other legal contexts. As more and more of such cases were decided, a mass of precedent was developed which could be used in later cases, even after the courts had become more conceptual, more rigidly logical, in their approach. The damage done to modern British administrative law by the survival of an obsolete principle of review was less in injustice to litigants than in a need for conceptual fuzziness to avoid injustice.

Nevertheless this confusion did leave room for injustice. With the growth of the welfare state in Britain, more and more aspects of a citizen's life became subject to government action and his need for a remedy against such injustice became more pressing. The passage of the Tribunals and Inquiries Act, 1958,[3] has eased matters, for it requires most administrative agencies to consent to review if an affected party asks for it before a decision is made, and to give reasons for their decision. But if a party fails to request such a "speaking order," either because he expects a favorable decision or because he does not know of the requirement, he may even now find himself bound by a "general order" which can only be reviewed on "jurisdictional" grounds, as before the act.

2 S. A. de Smith, *Judicial Review of Administrative Action* (London, 1959), p. 75. See the whole of his chapter 3 for a careful discussion of "jurisdiction" in this context.

3 Stat. 6 & 7 Eliz. 2, c. 66.

I

SUBJECT AND LOCAL OFFICIAL IN ELIZABETHAN ENGLAND

From about the thirteenth to the early sixteenth century, the role of government in English society grew only slowly. Henry VII's officials spent much of their time enforcing the legislation of Edward I and Edward III. There had been more change in the structure of government, but even here the rate of change had been slow enough so that, using traditional procedures in their endless task of defining the rights of citizens and officials alike, the courts could easily keep pace with the impact of new legislation.

With the Reformation and the economic changes of the sixteenth century, however, came an unprecedented increase in legislation, in response to a set of new problems to which legal procedures then in use were not well adapted. Thus the enclosure movement and the inflation of prices brought about by the influx of New World gold and silver led to unemployment and hordes of "sturdy beggars." When attempts to deal with these unfortunates by the accepted methods of criminal justice proved futile, the Elizabethan poor laws followed, imposing very substantial burdens on the landowner and giving wide discretion to the overseers of the poor (under the supervision of the justices of peace). The same demand for more pasture for sheep and cattle that led to enclosures led also to an increased interest in flood control and the draining of fen lands, and the sewers commissions were given more powers to undertake new works as well as to enforce long-established duties.

In these contexts as well as in other aspects of local government which will be discussed later, the old-fashioned remedies of damage suits against officials proved more and more of a hindrance to efficient government, and the need for new remedies became very plain. To make this state of affairs clearer, let us examine more closely some parts of the structure of local government in England about the year 1600, along with the remedies against officials that were available to the average substantial Englishman at that time.

Roughly speaking, such an Englishman was governed from three levels. At the top, in the central government, were the Crown, the Privy Council, and the great officers of state; Parliament; and the central courts of justice at Westminster: King's Bench, Common Pleas, Exchequer, and Chancery (with the Star Chamber acting as a court, though its close relation to the Privy Council was clearly visible). At the bottom level were many bodies of local government which were on the whole older than most of the central government itself. Township or vill, parish and manor, though theoretically distinguishable, were coterminous in most of rural England and their names were often interchanged even in the sixteenth century. In addition to these there were chartered boroughs, hundreds, specialized sewers commissions, and doubtless other bodies. Between top and bottom stood the county officials, sheriff, undersheriffs, and especially justices of peace—members of the local gentry who acted as intermediaries between central and local government.

Minor Criminal Justice

Fundamental responsibility for keeping the king's peace—the oldest activity of government—was shared among the three levels in a seemingly haphazard way which had "just growed" since Alfred's time, but which was more efficient than it looked. With major crimes, tried and punished in the central courts at Westminster, we cannot be here concerned. But minor criminal justice was in some measure the model for much other activity of local government.

At the base of the pyramid were the court leet of a manor (or village or township or parish) and its village constable. The court leet, an assembly of the householders in the township, was presided over by the steward of the lord of the manor. In law the steward acted as the king's judge, for Elizabethan lawyers considered that the leet's jurisdiction over petty crimes and misdemeanors had been originally granted by the crown. The leet's jurisdiction to inquire into wrongdoing was very wide, extending from treason and felony to such minor matters as infractions of the sumptuary laws. It was exercised through presentments of a jury chosen by the steward. A presentment was a simple statement under oath, by the jury collectively, in this form:

> The Jurors say upon their oath, that William Potter of Islington, Laborer, on such a day . . . feloniously took and carried away a black satin coat from the goods of James Anderson of Islington aforesaid.
>
> Also they present that Richard White is a common brewer

of drink, and brewed divers times unwholesome drink, and broke the assise.[1]

The jurors were to present every crime and misdemeanor that had been committed since the last court leet, according to their "charge" which was read to them by the steward. In 1623 the charge to the leet included thirty articles of felony and treason, and nearly fifty articles for lesser misdemeanors, as well as nearly twenty statutes of which violations were enquirable in the leet.[2] Generally speaking the leet jury presented "of its own knowledge," but at least by 1590 it sometimes heard evidence.[3]

The court leet had no power to try or punish treason or felony. Presentments of these crimes were to be written down and certified to the King's judges at the next assizes held in the county.[4] In lesser matters the steward as judge could order monetary penalties, either fines (assessed by the steward himself) or amercements (smaller payments, assessed by the homage of the court). He could also order punishment by means of the pillory, stocks, or ducking-stool, but he could not imprison.[5]

The leet's chief enforcement officer and usually the village's only police officer was the petty constable. Drawn from the lower ranks of society, he might be elected by the court leet, appointed by the steward of the lord of the manor, or chosen by some other custom. His service

1 The Assize of Bread and Ale, a price-control "statute" relating the prices of bread and ale to the price of grain, was enacted in 1266 and still actively enforced under Elizabeth I (and later).

2 John Kitchin, *Le Court Leete et Court Baron* (London, 1623), 8b-21.

3 *Wyld v. Cookman,* Cro. Eliz. 492 (K.B. 1596).

4 Kitchin, *Le Court Leete,* 8b.

5 *Richard Godfrey's Case,* 11 Co. 42 at 43b (K.B., 1614); *Stevenson v. Scrogs,* Moore 607 (K.B., 1597 or 1598).

was compulsory and must have been burdensome, as his oath shows:[6]

> You shall swear, That you will . . . indeavour that the Peace of our Soveraigne the Queen, well and truely according to your power, be kept, and you shall arrest all which you see making Riots, Debates, or Frayes, or breaking the Peace, and you shall well and truely indeavour your selves according to your knowledge, that the Statute of Winton for Watch, Hue and Cry, and the Statutes made for the punishment of sturdy Beggers, Vagabonds, Rogues, and other idle persons comming within your Office, that the Offenders be punished; and you shall indeavour your selves upon complaint to you, to apprehend Barretors, and riotous persons making Frayes, and also apprehend Felons, and if any of them make resistance . . . you shall make out-cry, and pursue them till they are taken, and you shall looke to such persons as use unlawful Games, and you shall have regard to the maintenance of Artillery, and you shall well and duely execute all Processe and Warrants sent unto you from the Justices of Peace of the County . . . and you shall well and duly, according to your power and knowledge, doe that which belongs to your Office of a Constable to doe, for this year to come.

A constable was required to pursue and arrest criminals, if possible, when he was given notice of a crime in his district. He was to arrest "suspected persons, which walk in the night and sleepe in the day" and to break up affrays or riots; to arrest those who "make assault upon any private persons" or break the peace in any other way. If he failed to make an arrest in a proper case he might be presented in the court leet or even indicted. But if he arrested without a warrant in an improper case, the aggrieved citizen could sue him in damages for his tres-

6 Kitchin, *Le Court Leete* (1623), 47 (in the 1653 edition, 93).

pass. Since it was not always clear what his legal duty was, his position was sometimes "damned if I do, and damned if I don't." Thus in *Stretton v. Browne*, the defendant constable had chosen the plaintiff to serve in the night watch, and arrested him when he refused. Justice Wray thought that he could lawfully do so, but Wray's colleague Justice Gawdy thought that he ought to complain to a justice of peace instead. When a constable arrested without warrant, even in a proper case, he had the burden of pleading and proving his authority to do so.[7]

In executing the judgments of a court leet, the constable acted on warrant from the seneschal or steward who had presided over the court. He could be sued at common law if he acted illegally, but if he had a warrant from the seneschal it was for the plaintiff to plead and prove any flaws in his authority.[8] Moreover, it seems that the plaintiff was not allowed to traverse (contradict) the facts alleged in the underlying presentment, unless the presentment laid a burden on freehold land.[9]

If, when the constable attempted to collect a fine or amercement, the defendant refused to pay, the usual procedure was to distrain or take possession of his cattle or other goods and keep them in the village pound until he did pay. The owner of the cattle could sue in the central courts in replevin for the return of the cattle, or in trespass for money damages. Here again, if a distraint was based on a presentment in the leet, the facts presented

7 *Stretton v. Browne*, Cro. Eliz. 204 (K.B., 1590). Cf. also *Beal v. Charter*, Cro. Eliz. 287 (K.B. 1592).

8 *Curteys' Case*, Moore 847 (K.B., 1615/16).

9 *Anonymous*, Dy. 13b (1536). That Justice Fitzherbert's dissent in this case probably was not law at that time appears from Y.B. 5 Hen. 7, fo. 4, pl. 9 (1489); but by 1699 it was said that all presentments in leets were traversable. *Groenvelt v. Burwell*, 1 Ld. Ray. 454 at 470 (dictum of Holt, C.J.).

could not be traversed, so that issue could be taken only on the regularity of the proceedings or the legality of the presentment. Thus in *Hall v. Turbett*, on replevin, it was held that the steward could not fine a man for not coming to court and doing his suit unless a jury had presented him. In *Evington v. Brimston* it was held that leaving gates open to the damage of the neighbors was not a wrong inquirable in the leet, and in *Wormleighton v. Burton* the same was said of letting geese onto the village common.[10]

The perils of a constable's life are well illustrated by the last two cases named. In both of them the constable distrained on a warrant regular in form and duly based on a presentment which, however, was for a matter beyond the court leet's powers. In *Wormleighton*, a replevin, the plaintiff merely won back his beasts that had been distrained. But in *Evington* the constable was made to pay damages for a wrong that was not his in the first place. Moreover, if he refused to execute the steward's warrants he might himself be fined in the leet or even be indicted before the justices of peace at their sessions.[11] In such cases it was the lowly constable who paid like an insurer for the illegality of the leet's actions. Yet it was a very exceptional constable who was learned in the law.

From the point of view of the aggrieved citizen, too, this state of affairs was less than satisfactory. True, in many cases he could recover against the constable whose action was not legally justified. But a constable was no more likely to be rich than to be learned, and there must

10 *Hall v. Turbett*, Cro. Eliz. 241 (C.B. 1591); *Evington v. Brimston*, Cro. Eliz. 414 (K.B. 1595); *Wormleighton v. Burton*, Cro. Eliz. 448 (C.B. 1595).

11 Kitchin, *Le Court Leete* (1623), 12; *Coleman's Case*, 2 Rol. Rep. 78 (K.B., 1619).

have been many cases in which suing him would be wasted effort.

A single justice or two justices acting outside the formal Sessions of the Peace also had an important part in keeping the king's peace. A single justice's most important power was, on proper complaint, to bind persons over to keep the peace or to be of good behavior, that is, to find security which would be forfeit if he broke the peace or otherwise breached the condition of his bond. He could also inquire into forcible entries into land, and order restitution of the land.[12] He could detain and examine suspicious persons,[13] order rioters and unlawful assemblies to disperse, order a "Rogue, Vagabond, or sturdie begger" to be whipped, and arrest poachers.[14]

Two justices of the peace acting out of the sessions could punish riots, and (among other things) could commit servants who refused to work or who took more than the legal wages, masters who paid more than the legal wages, and servants who assaulted their masters.[15]

In these matters the justice or justices might act either in person or by a warrant to the local constable. In the latter case, Lambard said, the constable ought not "to dispute whether their commandements be grounded upon sufficient authority or no: as knowing that although a Justice of the Peace (which is a Judge of Recorde) should direct a Warrant beyond his authoritie to a Constable . . . yet shall such Officer be holden excused for executing the same, howsoever that Justice of peace himselfe be blamed for it."[16] The justice himself might or might not be

12 William Lambard, *Eirenarcha* (London, 1610), Book II, c. 2, 3, 4.

13 *Scavage v. Tateham*, Cro. Eliz. 829 (C.B., 1601/02).

14 Lambard, *Eirenarcha*, Book II, c. 5; c. 7, pp. 200, 204.

15 *Ibid.*, Book III, c. 1.

16 William Lambard, *The Dueties of Constables* (London, 1599), pp. 19-20.

held liable in an action for damages based on an illegal warrant. For his actions done as judge "of record" he was not liable[17] and the aggrieved citizen was left with no remedy even though the justice had acted illegally. In other cases the law was less than clear. Where he issued a warrant to arrest that was not based on an accusation, he was held liable;[18] on the other hand, the court was divided in a case in which the justice had refused to take a statement from the plaintiff's servant who had witnessed a robbery, according to the statute of hue and cry.[19] Here also in some cases it would be the citizen aggrieved by illegal action who was out of luck. He had no remedy against the constable if the constable acted on warrant from a justice or higher authority, and he might not have any remedy against the justice either. Moreover, after 1609, by statute, if he sued either constable or justice and lost, he might lose double his costs for wrongful vexation.[20]

Justices of peace in their sessions could not only issue warrants to constables, like the justices acting out of Sessions, but they were also expected to oversee their activities as a whole. They could appoint constables in hundreds and parishes where no other choice had been made,[21] could remove "insufficient" constables[22] and could punish most forms of constabulary misbehavior.[23]

17 Cf. *Anonymous,* Y.B. 9 Edw. 4, fo. 3 (1468).

18 *Roger Windham v. Ed[ward] Clere,* Cro. Eliz. 130 (1588). There is no discussion of "probable cause" as such in the case.

19 *Green v. Hundred of Buccles-churches Case,* 1 Leon. 323, pl. 456 (1588) (dicta).

20 Stat. 7 Jac., c. 5 (1609).

21 1 *Warwick County Records: Sessions Orders* (Warwick, 1935) at 12, 17 (1625). Cf. *Constable of Homebey's Case,* 1 Mod. 13 (1669).

22 Lambard, *Duty of Constables,* p. 19.

23 Lambard, *Eirenarcha,* pp. 437, 438, 444, 475, 478, and elsewhere.

Other Local Administration

The Elizabethan government relied on the essentially criminal procedures of presentment and fine to carry out many public programs which would now be considered remote from criminal justice. In addition, many newer public programs based on taxation led up to the same ultimate enforcement—the constable with a warrant—and thus a citizen could have the same remedies against illegality as in criminal matters. All the inadequacies of common-law damage suits which we have already noted applied equally when they were used to test the legality of noncriminal public action. But here standards of legality were complex and constantly developing, so that the constable's burden of liability and harassment became ever heavier and less predictable. In such circumstances it is not surprising that attempts were made to discourage suits against officials, nor that citizens felt the need for a more efficient means of testing official action.

Public Works: Highways and Bridges

The roads of medieval and Elizabethan England were necessarily a local responsibility. Every parish was required to maintain the highways within its boundaries, through surveyors of highways named by a meeting of the inhabitants during Easter week. The surveyors were to name six days before the following Midsummer Day for work on the roads, and on those days every landowner was to send two men and a team, while other men were to come and work themselves.[24] If a man failed to do his share of the work or committed any of various other offenses in relation to the highways, the supervisors

24 Stat. 2 & 3 Phil. & M., c. 8; 5 Eliz. c. 13; 18 Eliz. c. 10.

were to present him to a single justice of peace, who in turn was to certify him at sessions. If he was convicted at the sessions, two justices (one "of the quorum") could issue a warrant to a constable or other officer to levy the forfeiture imposed at the sessions, and it was only at this stage that an aggrieved inhabitant could challenge the proceedings at law. A single justice could make presentment in the sessions if a parish failed to keep its roads in repair or failed to appoint any supervisor. The parish could also take other steps. Thus the parish of Anstye, Hertfordshire, pleaded:

that the said parish consisted of so few families, they were not able to repair the same, being two miles in length, by performing their ordinary days' work according to the statute, although they have in some years doubled their works, and therefore prayed to have some aid . . . from such parishes as stand chargeable to repair little or no part of any highways.
The Court referred the consideration thereof to the justices at their next Quarter Sessions to make some order therein, and at this present Sessions Sir Robert Chester, Sir Robert Ceaser, Thomas Hanchett and Simeon Bragrave, esquires, justices of the county, are desired to nominate which of the towns shall contribute towards the amending of said highways.[25]

Liability for the maintenance of bridges was sometimes a matter of ancient custom, and might rest on the owner of certain lands, or on a parish, hundred, town, or city. On failure to perform his obligation the person or body politic liable might be fined or amerced in the sessions. If it could not be ascertained what person or body politic was responsible by custom, bridges were to be repaired

25 5 *Hertfordshire County Records, Calendar of Sessions Books* (Hertford, 1928), at 36 (January 1623/4).

by the inhabitants of the county (or corporate town) where they were located. Four justices of the peace (one of the quorum) were empowered to call before them the constables of the whole county and, with their assent, to tax the inhabitants for this purpose. They were to appoint collectors of this tax for each hundred, and also surveyors to carry out the repairs. The collectors had power to distrain for nonpayment of the tax,[26] and at that stage the reluctant taxpayer could test the whole bridge-repairing program by suits in replevin or in damages.

Licensing of Alehouses

Another area in which the justices of peace had administrative powers was the licensing of "alehouses and tippling-houses"; this was to be done by two justices out of sessions, one "of the quorum." They were to take recognizances or bonds from the licensees against "the using of unlawfull games" and for "the using and maintenance of good order and rule" in the alehouses, and certify them to the sessions. The sessions then had power to inquire whether a licensee had kept the conditions of his bond, and to revoke his license.[27] But it seems that the bond itself could only be forfeited in the central courts at Westminster, so that the licensee automatically had the remedy of a new trial by a higher authority. Two justices out of sessions, one of the quorum, could commit anyone who kept an alehouse without license until he gave bond not to do so.

26 Stat. 22 Hen. 8, c. 5 (1531).

27 Stat. 5 & 6 Edw. 6, c. 25 (1552); 1 *Somerset Quarter Sessions Records*, (London, 1907), *passim*.

Laborers and Apprentices

The enforcement provisions of the Elizabethan Statutes of Laborers[28] gave wide powers to the justices and other local government officials, enforced generally by criminal penalties. For instance, servants were to be hired from year to year, and were not to leave before the end of the term without obtaining permission from two justices of peace (or the mayor of a corporate town). A master who fired his servant without sufficient cause before the end of his term was to be fined forty shillings in the sessions, the assizes, or the mayor's court. A servant who left before his year was up could be committed to prison by the mayor or two justices of peace until he gave bond to serve out the rest of his term. Similar penalties applied to masters who fired servants, even at the end of the year, without a quarter's warning, and to servants who left without giving notice or who refused to work for the legal wages. No servant was to leave his parish to seek work elsewhere without written license from the mayor or constable, under penalty of being whipped as a vagabond. The justices at their Easter sessions were to set wage scales for laborers, husbandmen, and various other occupations. Masters who paid more than the wages set could be imprisoned for ten days by a single justice; two justices out of sessions could send servants who took higher wages to jail for 21 days. Other provisions regulated apprenticeships and compulsory work at harvest time.

The only important provision which was not enforced by some form of criminal penalty was that which authorized a single justice of peace (or the mayor of a

28 Stat. 5 Eliz., c. 4 (1563).

corporate town) to hear complaints as between master and apprentice and "by his wisdome and discretion, take such order and direction betweene the said Master and his Apprentice as the equitie of the cause might require." In a proper case he could discharge the parties from their agreement.

Against all such orders except the last-named, it will be noted, the injured subject had at least a theoretical remedy. He could sue the constable who executed the order for unlawfully taking his goods (in the case of a monetary penalty) or for false imprisonment. But the master or apprentice who conceived himself ill-used by an order dissolving their agreement had no sufficient remedy.

Poor Law; Bastardy

The function which took most time, money, and effort from Elizabethan local government was probably the care of the poor. Each parish's responsibility for its poor was first stated in the statute 27 Henry 8, c. 25 (1536) but it was not until the last years of Queen Elizabeth that the parish was given power to tax the inhabitants instead of relying on alms.[29] The churchwardens, who as the business managers of a parish had administered parish charities, were to appoint two or more substantial householders to serve with them as overseers; but they often appointed only themselves, and it was held that this was permissible.[30]

The overseers were then to set rates for the relief of the poor, to collect them with the aid of the town or

29 Stat. 43 Eliz., c. 2 (1601).

30 *Gollope's Case*, Harvard Law School MS (Turner) 106, fo. 430 (K.B., 1631).

parish constable, and to disburse them as needed. If a taxpayer refused to pay, the overseers could levy on and sell his goods after obtaining a warrant from two justices of peace. A taxpayer aggrieved by the overseer's actions could complain to the justices of peace in quarter sessions,[31] or he could wait until his goods were levied on and sue in trespass. The officer who levied a tax illegally assessed was liable in damages even though he acted on a warrant regular in form.[32] But the aggrieved citizen who sued in such cases must take a very substantial risk, for if he lost or was nonsuited the defendant officer could recover treble damages against him.[33]

Like the constable, the churchwardens and overseers of the poor looked to the justices of peace for support and supervision. A single justice could appoint overseers if the churchwardens had not done so, and could also rate the parish for the poor, levy the tax, and commit recalcitrant taxpayers if the churchwardens had not acted. He could order a "rogue" punished and sent to his last legal abode for relief. Two justices (one of the quorum) were to approve the churchwardens' choice of overseers, and to receive and approve the overseers' accounts at the end of the year. If the overseers refused to give accounts the same two justices had power to commit them. If a parish had not sufficient resources to take care of its poor, two justices could tax other parishes in the same hundred for its assistance. Poor rates were customarily collected by the churchwardens and overseers after service at the church door, but as had been mentioned, two justices

31 Stat. 43 Eliz., c. 2, paragraph 6.

32 *Nichols v. Walker and Carter*, Cro. Car. 394 (K.B., 1634).

33 Stat. 43 Eliz., c. 2, paragraph 20; *Brampton's Case*, 1 Rol. Rep. 272 (K.B., 1615).

could issue warrants to levy on the goods of recalcitrant ratepayers, and to commit those who refused to pay. Two justices could also approve the overseers' orders for binding poor children as apprentices.

Two or more justices in their general quarter sessions —meetings held at stated times for the execution of their general authority to enquire, hear, and determine all things within their power—could do various other things under the poor law. If a whole hundred had not the resources to relieve its poor, the quarter sessions could tax other parishes and hundreds to that end. They could also assess the parents, grandparents, and children of poor persons to contribute to their support.

Illegitimate children were the parish's responsibility under the poor law, unless they were otherwise provided for. Two justices out of sessions (one of the quorum) could make orders punishing either or both parents, and ordering the father to pay either the parish or the child's mother specified amounts for its care.[34]

A most important clause, from our point of view, was the provision "that if any person or persons shall find themselves grieved with any Sesse or Tax, or other act done by the sayd Churchwardens and other persons, or by the sayd Justices of Peace, that then it shall be lawfull for the Justices of Peace, at their generall quarter Sessions . . . to take such order therin, as shall be thought convenient, And the same to conclude and bind all the sayd parties."[35] This provision gave the poor their only effective remedy against arbitrary acts of the overseers, and some justices were very conscientious in hearing their complaints. Review by the sessions under this clause was

34 Stat. 18 Eliz. c. 3 (1576).
35 Stat. 43 Eliz., c. 2 (1601).

intended to be the only remedy for any party aggrieved, apparently to the exclusion of common-law damage suits. It was the development of certiorari that enabled parishes and taxpayers who could afford it to carry their complaints further to the King's Bench at Westminster.

Control of the Justices of Peace by the Privy Council

As we have seen, the suit for civil damages had (and still has) serious defects as a means of controlling official actions, even when it was available. But to avoid leaving a misleading impression, it should be pointed out that most officials and especially the justices of peace were subject to constant scrutiny by the central executive, the King in Council.

From the Council, the justices received a continual flow of orders and recommendations. For the year 1613-14, for instance, the *Acts of the Privy Council* contain ten or more communications to justices of peace concerning pensions to be granted to named veterans, two concerning procurement of timber for the navy, four pressing the King's need for voluntary contributions of money (for James I was nearly as determined to govern without Parliament as his son), and two calling for vigorous prosecution of "idle and vagrant persons" by whom robberies and burglaries are committed. Occasionally the Council also intervened in individual cases by nonjudicial means. For example: in 1613-1614 proctors of the University of Cambridge searched the village of Chesterton and were indicted for riot before the justices of peace of the county. The Privy Council "declared and adjudged" "that the said village of Chesterton is within the jurisdiction of the said University of Cambridge . . . For which consideration it was ordered that his Majesty's Atturney General should presently take a course for the stay of all proceedinges upon or by collour of the said inditement."[36] But it should be noted that here the directive is addressed not to the justices, but to the prosecution.

The Privy Council seems also to have issued some directives to the justices in the nature of rules of decision. In the records of the quarter sessions of the West Riding, Yorkshire, are preserved a series of "Directions from the Justices of Assize to the Justice of Peace," with the preamble, "My Lords the Justices of Assize do desire the Justices of Peace of his Countie to observe these directions hereafter ensuing, that their Lordships may have an accompt thereof att the next Assize, *because they are thereof to render an accompt to the Kinge.*"[37] The directions that follow deal with all phases of law enforcement: presentment, prosecution, and (less often) the punishments to be imposed.

In their capacity as judges the justices of peace also received guidance from the justices of assize. This was done in two ways. The commission of the peace provided that if a difficult case should come before a single justice, two justices, or more, "then you shall not proceed to give judgment (unless in the presence . . . of one of our Justices assigned to take assizes in the aforesaid county)."[38] The usual procedure when a case was felt to be difficult was to adjourn it until the next assizes and consult with the judge, who then stated the rules of law applicable. A

36 *Acts of the Privy Council,* 1613-14, pp. 84-85.

37 Yorkshire Archaeological Society, *Record Series,* vol. LIV, p. 397 (16 Jac., 1618). Emphasis mine.

38 Lambard, *Eirenarcha,* Book I, c. 8, p. 38 and c. 9, pp. 49-50.

typical case of this kind is *Villa de Tewksbury against Villa de Twyning*[39] which shows also something of the attitude of the parish officers toward a grievous social problem:

> Before the Judges of Assize this Case came in question . . . A servant Maid dwelling in *Twining* was there got with childe, and she being near the time of her Delivery, by practice she was conveyed out of the Parish of *Twining*, unto an Out-house or Hovel . . . which Hovel was near *Twining*, but within the Parish of *Tewksbury*, being the uttermost Confines of it, and there the childe was born: Afterwards the Parish of *Twining* gave relief unto her, and the Minister of *Twining* did Christen the Childe, and afterwards when she was able to remove, they of . . . *Twining* did receive her with the Childe, and gave relief to her for two years; afterwards the Mother being sick, they of *Twining* did send her away with the Childe to *Longden* . . . where the mother dyed; . . . then they of *Twyning* sent the Childe, being under the age of three years, unto the Ville of *Tewksbury*, within which Parish the Childe was borne, and they sent the childe again unto *Twyning*.
>
> The question, upon all this moved to the Judges, was, whether of these two Parishes . . . were to keep this Childe, and provide for it.
>
> Sir William Jones, before whom this was moved legally and regularly [held that Twining must keep the child, "the practice being very apparent" to have it born elsewhere.]

This advisory activity seems to have led naturally enough to general consultations among the royal judges and thus to agreement on general "resolutions" stating the law in these matters.[40] As the West Riding document

39 2 Bulstr. 349 (8 Car., 1632).

40 See e.g., *Resolutions concerning Inns,* Hutton 99, made at "a conference at Serjeants Inn in Fleet-Street," in June 22 Jac., 1624.

above cited shows, the judges must also have conferred with the Privy Council at times.

The Council usually exercised its control over officials with due regard for the law, but it often had other and more immediate interests to pursue. And though an aggrieved individual citizen could and often did complain to the Council, this was not an appropriate forum for most such grievances. In one instance the Council made a systematic and fairly successful attempt, however, to hear all complaints of citizens, to keep such complaints out of the common-law courts, and to follow different legal standards from the courts in the interests of efficient administration. This was the remarkable story of the sewers commissioners, the flood control and drainage bodies of Elizabethan and Stuart England.

Sewers Commissions

The sewers commissions were appointed from the local gentry of every county by the Lord Chancellor, the Lord Treasurer, and the two chief justices. Usually the lists of commissioners overlapped the list of justices of peace, for the two groups came from the same social background. Their function was "to survey the walles, streames, ditches, bankes, gutters, sewers, gotes, calcies [causeways], bridges . . . and the same cause to be made, corrected, repaired, amended, put down and reformed."[41]

They used procedures much like a court leet's and they were always considered a court of record, although to modern eyes the commissions look much like a true

41 Stat. 23 Hen. 8, c. 5 (1532-33). This was a consolidation and development of the statute 6 Hen. 6, c. 5 (1427-28). The new statute put less emphasis on proceeding by "the oaths of lawful men" and more on what they should do "by their wisdoms and discretions," but otherwise it gives much the same powers.

administrative agency. Typically they proceeded as follows. A jury of twelve men was summoned by the sheriff for each convenient territorial unit under the commissioners' supervision. After the jurors had been sworn they proceeded to view all the dikes, ditches, sea walls, and the like in their area, and then made formal presentments before the commissioners. A typical presentment by such a jury reads, "Item we present Elizabethe norton widdow to amend coope and mak upp higher xv roddes of hire walle againste the rivere of Thames before allhalloutide next uppon paine of everye rodd not don & to be made higher xii d alhalloutide."[42] When the time for completing the work had passed, the jury would again view the locale and make a second presentment of any defaults. The jurors functioned like a medieval inquest: besides viewing the site, they regularly heard evidence and sometimes even argument of counsel before making their presentment,[43] but their activities before the presentment were not matter of record. It was always for the jury to determine who was liable to make a particular repair—like bridge repairs, a matter of immemorial custom—though the commissioners might decide on their own view what work ought to be done.[44]

It seems probable that in medieval times presentments made before sewers commissioners could not be traversed or contradicted before the commissioners. So late as 1576 we find a litigant asking leave to traverse and having his request refused.[45]

42 London County Council, *Court Minutes of the Surrey and Kent Sewers Commission* (London, 1909), p. 64.

43 *Ibid.*, p. 69, item 271; p. 183, item 683.

44 Robert Callis, *Reading upon the Statute of Sewers* (given in 1622 at Gray's Inn; published in London, 1647), pp. 82, 83.

45 London County Council, *Surrey and Kent Commission*, pp. 283-285.

The sewers commissions had power to collect money on the basis of the jury's presentments, and to enforce their orders by distress, amercement, and in some cases imprisonment. Money so collected could then be spent on the repairs as necessary. The commissioners had power to appoint bailiffs, surveyors, collectors, and expenditors as needed; to hire workmen; to take carts, horses, and oxen; and "to do all things requisite." Like other local officials, these functionaries could be sued at common law; and they had roughly the same defenses available to them. In medieval times a citizen could also, if he wished, have a presentment against him removed from the "Court of Sewers" to the King's Bench by writ of certiorari, and could there have a trial de novo of both the facts in the presentment and the lawfulness of the commissioners' action. This use of certiorari was common in medieval times, but had lapsed sometime before 1585, possibly with a statute of 1531.[46]

During the sixteenth century a new interest in draining low lands appeared, calling for new public works on an ever larger scale. This interest is reflected in the statute 23 Henry 8, c.5, which laid new emphasis on what the commissioners might do without a jury. The new projects called for much exercise of the commissioners' "wisdoms and discretions." The first large new project described by Dugdale[47] was two great "sewers" (ditches) twenty feet wide, five feet deep, and at least two miles long, ordered in 1542 by Charles Duke of Suffolk and his fellow commissioners of sewers for the parts of Kesteven and Holland in Lincolnshire. The

46 Controlment Rolls, King's Bench, *passim.*

47 William Dugdale, *History of Imbanking and Draining of Divers Fens and Marshes* (London, 1772), pp. 203-204.

Privy Council began to take an interest in projects for draining the fenlands of East Anglia in 1576,[48] but did not intervene on a large scale until the turn of the century.

In 1601 a General Draining Act[49] was passed by Parliament authorizing holders of common rights in the "drowned lands" to contract with private "undertakers" for draining them, and giving a majority of commoners in any area power to bind the whole group. Both the private undertakers and the commissioners of sewers seem to have had shares in the great drainage projects of this period: their exact relationship is not clear, nor is it important for our purposes. One project under this act, begun in 1605, affected over 300,000 acres or nearly 480 square miles. The undertakers (who included Sir John Popham, then Lord Chief Justice of England, and his successor Sir Thomas Fleming) were to have 130,000 acres "to be taken out of the worst sort of every particular Fen proportionably," in return for their performance, giving them a powerful incentive toward good work.[50] The dike known as Popham's Eau resulted from this project; but the draining of the fens was not completed successfully until Cromwell's time, under the direction of the Earl of Bedford.

There was much local opposition to the drainage projects. "Divers perverse-spirited people" brought "turbulent suits in law, as well against the said commissioners as those whom they employed therein," and made "libellous songs to disparage the work."[51] Dugdale says that

48 *Acts of the Privy Council*, 1575-1577, p. 134.

49 Stat. 43 Eliz., c. 11 (1601).

50 Dugdale, *Imbanking and Draining*, pp. 383f.

51 *Ibid.*, p. 391. For a "libellous song" see Appendix E.

the work on the Great Level of East Anglia was completely stopped on this account for five years, but the record of the *Acts of the Privy Council* suggests that his statement is exaggerated. In any case, it was not long before the opposition led to a head-on collision between the Privy Council and the common-law courts.

In 1609 the Council asked the common-law justices for an advisory opinion on a decree ordering a new channel built for the river Ouse. The justices, perhaps led by Coke, gave as their opinion that sewers commissioners had no authority to make such a new river, though they might make slight changes in the course of an existing river. They said also that taxes imposed by the commissioners could not be assessed against a vill as a whole but must be apportioned among the inhabitants for whose benefit the work was undertaken, according to the amount of their land.[52] Five years later, the commissioners of sewers for the county of Northampton assessed a fine upon a certain village as a whole and ordered that all of it be levied upon the cattle of one William Hetley. The cattle were sold and Hetley brought an action at law for them; he was imprisoned by the commissioners when he refused to release his suit. He then brought habeas corpus in the King's Bench and was freed, while the commissioners were fined and committed "For it was held, that the Warrant by them made was in direct opposition to the Authority and Judgment of this Court" (citing *Rooke's Case*).[53] But his victory over the commissioners remained

52 *Case of the Isle of Ely*, 10 Co. 141 (Mich., 7 Jac., 1609). *Rooke's Case*, 5 Co. 99b (Hil., 40 Eliz., 1597/98), had held that all those who benefit by a repair must be taxed to pay for it, not only the owner of the land next to the river.

53 *Hetley v. Boyer & Mildmay et al.*, Cro. Jac. 336 (Hil., 11 Jac., 1613/14).

incomplete. When he sued them for false imprisonment[54] the Privy Council intervened, committed him, and forced him to release his action.[55]

The Council then (November 8, 1616) issued an elaborate order on this subject, drawn by Francis Bacon as Attorney General. It argues that the sewers commissioners do have power to construct new public works, to charge towns and hundreds that benefit by them as units without apportioning the taxes to individual landowners, and to commit "persons refractary and disobedient to their orders, warrantes and decrees." It then provides that persons who had already been committed by the Council for bringing suits against sewers commissioners or their officers "shall stand committed until they release or sufficyently discharge such accions, suites and demaundes . . . saving unto them, neverthelesse, any complaynt or suit for any oppression or greevance before the Court of Sewers, or before this Table, if they receive not justice at the Commissioners' handes."[56]

From 1616 until not long before 1639 the Council seems to have pursued the double-barreled policy indicated in this order. It took action regularly against anyone who sued sewers commissioners or their officers, and forced him to release his suit. At the same time it called upon those with grievances against the commissioners to complain, first to the commissioners themselves, and then to the Council. The records of the Council from 1616 to 1628 show five occasions on which they intervened to force release of suits against sewers

54 *Headley v. Sir Anthony Mildmay*, 1 Rol. Rep. 395 (Trin., 14 Jac., 1616).

55 *Acts of the Privy Council*, 1616-17, p. 240.

56 *Ibid.*, p. 57.

commissioners.[57] (In several other instances recalcitrants were summoned before the Council, but a lawsuit is not specifically mentioned.[58]) In the same period, on at least six occasions the Council held hearings and took action on behalf of citizens aggrieved by actions of sewers commissioners.[59]

It was perhaps in this connection and at this time that Oliver Cromwell, then of Ely, first put himself in opposition to government by the royal prerogative. For "it was commonly reported by the commoners of Ely Fens, and the fens adjoining, that Mr. Cromwell, of Ely, had undertaken, they paying him a groat for every cow they had upon the common, to hold the drainers in suit of law for five years, and that in the meantime they should enjoy every foot of their common."[60]

But the reports and records that have been examined indicate that the Council was quite successful in keeping damage suits against sewers commissioners out of the common-law courts.[61] Since, as has been noted, the courts' removal jurisdiction over them by certiorari had lapsed some time before 1585, it seems that during this period the Privy Council was the sole recourse of parties aggrieved by acts of sewers commissioners.

Thus for most actions of local government the subject's only remedy was a suit for civil damages against

57 *Acts of the Privy Council*, 1616-17, pp. 44, 128; 1621-23, pp. 95, 239; 1625-26, pp. 64, 463.

58 *Ibid.*, 1616-17, pp. 39, 54.

59 *Ibid.*, 1616-17, pp. 75, 83, 294; 1618-19, pp. 161, 205; 1623-25, pp. 181, 287.

60 *Calendar of State Papers*, Domestic, 1631-33, p. 501.

61 There is only one damage suit among the reported cases: *Thursbie v. Warren*, Benloe 199 (Mich., 2 Car., 1626). None were found in the Controlment Rolls of King's Bench nor in such King's Bench plea rolls as were examined. However, actions involving particular types of defendants are less easily picked out from the rolls than original writs of a particular type, and the records of the Common Bench were not examined.

the constable or other enforcing officer. These suits imposed an intolerable burden on the lowest-ranking local officials, who were unlikely to be learned in the law. At the same time they could hinder the flexible operation of government when a new program was to be carried out. Consequently Parliament passed statutes limiting their availability and imposing penalties on unsuccessful plaintiffs, while in one important area the Privy Council intervened to prevent aggrieved citizens from exercising their legal right to sue at all. Moreover, at best damage suits were not available to test much government activity, since they did not lie against justices of peace for their judicial actions, whether criminal or merely administrative in nature. Finally it should be pointed out that a damage suit comes long after the illegality has been executed, and gives a monetary remedy which may or may not be adequate.

The Corporate Towns

The legal position of a town dweller was not unlike that of his rural contemporary, for the town authorities generally had all the powers of courts leet, justices of peace, and surveyors of highways, as well as all the other statutory powers which have been described. Similarly the towns employed constables and other ministers, and the same common-law remedies in damages were available against them. But a town usually had other powers as well; and all its powers were exercised through a very different governmental structure.

Structure

No two corporate towns were exactly alike, for each had gained its "liberties" by a long process of bargaining with the Crown, or claimed them by immemorial custom.

Moreover, the lack of any comprehensive study of borough institutions at this time means that no generalization can be more than a preliminary guess. But in nearly all of them, by the sixteenth century, effective power was wielded by a mayor and a small council, chosen for life and known variously as the aldermen, the mayor's brethren, the capital burgesses, and other names as well. The evidence suggests that originally in some towns the aldermen may have been each associated with one of the craft guilds (Beverly), and in other towns each with one of the wards into which the town was divided (Leicester). By the end of the century the body of mayor and aldermen was usually self-perpetuating, the incumbents having power to fill vacancies as they occurred. It is only fair to add that the mayor and aldermen usually taxed themselves more heavily than anyone else in the borough.

With the mayor and aldermen was associated a larger body called the comburgesses, common council, or other such names, created fairly recently to represent the "commonalty" (the free burgesses of the town). But by 1600 its members were usually chosen directly or indirectly by the mayor and aldermen, who in any case had full power to decide when and whether they would consult the inferior body in the town's business. "The council" in these towns meant the mayor and aldermen, on some occasions with the common council and on others without them. Often the mayor and aldermen were constituted a court of record, with power to try civil disputes among the townsmen and criminal cases of all kinds; in these judicial powers the common council usually had no share.

Thus, for instance, Oxford in 1562 had a mayor,

twelve assistants, and twenty-four associates. Only the four senior assistants were called aldermen. The mayor was to be chosen for a year from among the assistants: three names were to be chosen "by the auncyenth being xxiiii^th^ to the foreseid xiii^th^" (perhaps meaning the twelve senior associates) from among the Twelve (assistants); two of the three names were then to be chosen by lot and the commons were to elect one of the two. Bailiffs (tax collectors) and chamberlains (keepers of accounts) were chosen by a similar procedure. The Twelve and the Twenty-Four (associates) were to be chosen by the then-existing town council "owte of the most awncyent, wyseste, and discreteste persons as to the seid Mr. Mayer and the xii shalbe thowght good, beinge nowe of the Counseyll of the same." Each man as he was elected was to join with the council in choosing the next.[62] The actual governing of the city was done by "the council," a body which sometimes consisted only of the mayor and the Twelve, and sometimes included the Twenty-four. The mayor and the four aldermen sat as judges in the mayor's court, but the jurisdiction of that court varied greatly from time to time, depending on the political strength of the university (with its rival court for suits of and by members of the university community). Poor relief appears to have been administered by the council for the town as a whole rather than by the individual parishes.

In Leicester there were a mayor; twenty-four "aldermen," "masters," or "mayor's brethren"; and a council of forty-eight known as "comburgesses" or "commonty" who were chosen by the mayor and aldermen. Each alder-

62 *Selections from the Records of the City of Oxford*, ed. W. H. Turner (Oxford, 1880), pp. 290, 292.

man had administrative duties in a ward of a city, as to inspect inns and alehouses. The council as a body (again sometimes including the comburgesses and sometimes not) chose constables and "thridboroughs" whose duty it was to make presentments in the court held by the corporation every Monday (a court of record). The mayor, the recorder or town counsel, and the four aldermen who last had been mayor were justices of peace to enforce the statutes of vagabonds, of artificers, and of laborers.[63]

Reading in about 1600 had a mayor, seven capital burgesses (eight counting the mayor), and thirteen secondary burgesses. The mayor was chosen by the capital burgesses from among themselves. He served for a year, appointing the constables and wardens for each ward of the city, and was a justice of the peace for the city. The capital burgesses filled any vacancies arising among themselves, while the whole corporation chose the secondary burgesses. The mayor and the capital and secondary burgesses were magistrates of the borough court.[64]

Bylaws: Remedies against Town Officials

In the nature of urban living the town dweller was governed more than the countryman. Both rural leet and borough council usually had the power to make bylaws or ordinances; but as always, more people living closer together created more problems for collective solution. In addition, most boroughs had bought or otherwise acquired special privileges in connection with their

63 3 *Records of the Borough of Leicester* (1509-1603), M. Bateson, ed. (Cambridge, 1905) xxv, 363.

64 2 *Records of the Borough of Reading*, J. M. Guilding, ed. (London, 1895), *passim*.

markets and fairs. Craft guilds or chartered companies for each trade or occupation in the borough usually had similar powers. Thus the Leicester charter of 1599 empowers the mayor and aldermen "to grant and make from time to time such laws and regulations as shall seem to them useful and salutary, for the good government of the inhabitants and artificers of the borough, both for the victualling of the borough and for the disposal of lands given to the mayor, bailiffs and burgesses." "We will that no merchant or any man who is not a freeman of the borough may use any trade nor buy or sell other than in gross, except only in fair time, unless he has obtained the license of the Mayor, bailiffs and burgesses."[65]

Bylaws passed under these provisions touched on the burgess' common rights in the town's south fields, sale of bread and gloves in the town by "foreign" (non-Leicestrian) bakers and glovers, Sabbath observance, the supply of tallow for candles, weighing of wool for market at the Wool Hall, taxation of the borough, a stock of coal laid in at the Town Hall to be sold to the poor, provision of "leyther buckittes" (for fire-fighting) by the aldermen each for his ward, repair of pavements, standard weights and measures for use in the town market, and many other matters. In addition every borough had customs of long standing, perhaps based on bylaws which had been lost, as varied and almost as comprehensive as the municipal bylaws.

These bylaws and customs might be enforced by fine or amercement, followed by levy of goods; by distraint; or by an action of debt in the royal courts (for a mone-

65 3 *Leicester Records* 361, 363.

tary penalty of more than 40 shillings). Except in the last case an aggrieved citizen could sue the enforcing officer for damages for any unlawful act, whether the illegality lay in the custom or bylaw or in his own actions. Here again the constable or searcher was made an insurer, and the citizen was protected only at his expense.

The law governing the officer's actions in these cases was far from clear. Chief Justice Coke thought, for instance, that a town could not imprison for violation of a bylaw, though it could fine or disfranchise the offender.[66] But the town of Leicester had authority to imprison expressly given in the 1599 charter, and we have no case to show whether such a grant was valid. Early in the sixteenth century imprisonment for violation of bylaws seems to have been taken for granted.[67]

In a very general way the criteria for valid municipal bylaws are stated in the paragraph of Leicester's charter which has been quoted. But there were innumerable relevant considerations in applying these general standards to a particular custom or bylaw. Thus in *Hill v. Haukes* the bellman of Lichfield took from every person who sold grain in the market-place a pint of grain if he offered a bushel or less for sale, a quart of grain if he offered more than one bushel, for the benefit of the Corporation of Lichfield. As to the custom itself, it seems not good, the plaintiff argued,

> because it is unreasonable to have so much from everyone who brings a bushel for sale . . . for this is a large profit . . . also it is not reasonable that the Bellman should have the

66 *Clarkes Case,* 5 Co. 64 (1596), said to be the same case as *Bab v. Clerke,* Moore 411 (1595) *sed quaere,* which see.

67 For example, 1 *Reading Records* 188-189, 244; *Oxford City Records,* pp. 289, 414.

benefit of this, and that he being a person of low degree should have the ransacking of every man's sack . . . And *Coke* and *Dodderidge* [JJ.] the Corporation is at much expense to repair the road, and thus it is for the benefit of those who bring their corn to the market, also the Bellman is merely the servant of the Corporation, and they have the profit and bear the expense, and if there are twenty bushels he shall have only a quart. [Judgment was given for the defendant bellman.][68]

In *Davenant v. Hurdis*[69] the company of Merchant Tailors in London had made a bylaw that their members should give half their cloth-working business to members of their own guild. Coke, then Attorney General, argued against the bylaw "a general rule in by-laws . . . that they must be *per majorem partem* . . . And by-laws must have their ground in custom, consent or royal letters patent." Citing Y.B. 44 Edward 3 fo. 18, he argued "that by-laws for pavements and other works necessary to carry on the public business, as highways, causeys and the like, are binding without a custom, but they must always be made *per majorem partem*. And a royal patent is a good warrant to make by-laws, if they are not in oppression of the subject, but by-laws that sound in oppression are not warrantable by patent." He argued further that this by-law applied only to members of the company—for plaintiff was not a member—and that it was unreasonable as tending to create a monopoly. He won his case on the last ground.

In *The Chamberlain of London's Case*,[70] however, an ordinance requiring all cloth to be inspected at Black-

68 1 Rol. Rep. 1, 44 (1614). The bellman's job was to sweep the marketplace.
69 Moore 576 (1599).
70 5 Co. 62b (1590).

well Hall to see whether it was saleable, and to pay a penny for each cloth, was upheld as reasonable.

As these cases serve to illustrate, when a municipal officer acted to enforce a bylaw or custom, his liability in damages might depend on subtle and complicated judgments of fact. Questions of law might also arise, as in *Heddy v. Wheelhouse*.[71] Here the bailiff of Northampton distrained a cow for nonpayment of toll at a fair, and the question on which the case turned was whether the words of a charter of King Henry VII authorized taking this toll. Thus it may be seen that however difficult was the position of a rural constable, a municipal officer ran even greater risks in the execution of his duty.

Borough Franchise

Neither the "freemen" or "free burgesses" nor the other inhabitants of corporate towns had any right to choose the members of the corporation or to be consulted in the town's business, though they might in fact be consulted on occasion. In many towns their only means of expressing grievances was by presentments in the borough court as in a court leet.[72] Nevertheless, the effect of the borough charter and the town bylaws was to give the free burgess a specially favored economic position which was well worth having. Members of the craft guilds or chartered companies, the largest group of free burgesses, had the exclusive right to carry on their trades within the borough: a "stranger" from any other part of England could work as a journeyman, or could occa-

71 Cro. Eliz. 558 (1596).

72 Cf. 4 *Records of the Borough of Nottingham* (1547-1625) (Nottingham, 1889), 112-113, for a presentment of "you, Maister Mayre" and another of an alderman, as well as two petitions to the mayor.

sionally buy the freedom of the town for a price; but if he set up shop for himself without permission he would be fined heavily and warned away. Strangers could buy and sell in the town market held once or twice a week, but the free burgesses claimed the right to act as middlemen between them. Town bylaws often forbade strangers to sell to any but freemen, or to buy from one another.[73]

There were three ways of becoming free of a borough. Probably the most common method was by serving an apprenticeship of seven years to a master who was himself a freeman. The son of a freeman was automatically entitled to the franchise of the borough. And in some boroughs strangers were sometimes allowed to buy their freedom by paying a fairly heavy fine. In some towns the craft guilds apparently passed on admissions to the franchise, but more often this was done by the mayor and council, however constituted.

"Thordre for the admyssion of Fremen" passed in 1551 by the mayor, aldermen, and council of Oxford "wyth the concent of the more part of thenhabytants of the seyd Cytye" may serve as an example.

Item, that every prentyce servying hys master the hole terme of vii yeres or more accordying to hys covenants expressed yn hys indenturs, well and truly as a prentyce owght to do, shall at thend of the same terme be presentyd by hys master and ii of thoccupacion that he is of unto Master Mayar . . . yn the Guyld hall att the court tyme, and the seyd prentice there yn the face of the court to be sworne and made fre of the guyld of the seyd Cytye, and to pay for the copye of hys fredom iiiis. vid. forthwythe wythowt any further delay, as before ys seyd.

73 For example, 3 *Leicester Records* 44, 154, 406; 4 *Nottingham Records* 254, 255, 308.

One son of a freeman could be presented to the Mayor by his father and be admitted for the same four shillings, sixpence, which was divided among various officials of the town. More sons than one could be admitted on payment of an extra nine shillings, sixpence.

Other persons "shall furste before he or they be admytted to be fre, desyer the good wyll of the crafte or occupacion that he or they wyll fre of, and pay unto theym xs. and a brekefaste for hys admyssion ynto the seyd craft or occupacion; and the seyd person and persons to be presented . . . by the Master and Wardens, or some two or iii persons of the seyd occupacon to the Mayar and Councell of the seyd Cytye" paying four shillings, sixpence, in petty fees and at least five pounds to the use of the whole of the city. Occasionally, however, a man whose friendship to the city was desired was admitted for a lesser fine.[74]

A burgess could be disfranchised by the mayor and council for many reasons. Nonresidence in the borough or failure to pay borough taxes, disobedience to borough bylaws, and contempt to the mayor or aldermen are some of the causes given in the records. He might also be restored by the same body, usually on paying a fine and making submission. But before 1600 he had no remedy against the corporation's decision, even though the decision might be based on factional politics.

In the towns as in country areas, then, the citizen aggrieved by actions of government officials lacked an adequate or easily available remedy for his wrong. The problem was the more acute in the towns because town

74 *Oxford City Records*, p. 204.

life inherently requires more regulation. The complexities of town bylaws placed an intolerable burden on the enforcing officer who paid like an insurer if the bylaw was held to be unreasonable. Moreover, in the important matter of the borough franchise a townsman had no remedy at all. The need was clear, therefore, for new remedies which would allow citizens to test the legality of official activity without either hampering necessary government programs or overburdening minor officials.

II

MANDAMUS: ORIGINS

Of the two new remedies against governmental action which developed in the seventeenth century mandamus came first. It appeared originally as a "writ of restitution" to a borough franchise, when a freeman claimed to have been unjustly deprived of his freedom. This, as we have noted, was an area in which the citizen had no remedy at all; readers learned in the law will note that this is only one example of the nearly total lack in the common law system of any remedy designed to make government officials take positive action, no matter how good a right the plaintiff might have to that action.

Legal tradition usually picks up the story of mandamus with *James Bagge's Case*, the outcome of a bitter squabble among the burgesses of Plymouth in Devon. James Bagge, a capital burgess of the town, "conducted himself contemptuously and scurrilously both in words and gestures" toward one mayor after another (as the mayor told the story). He called mayor Robert Trelawney "a cozening knave" and Thomas Sherwill "a seditious fellow." He "seditiously and maliciously incited and persuaded" one of his colleagues to conspire with him to remove another mayor, saying "Maister Maior carrieth himselfe foolishly in his place . . . wee will turne him out of his Maioraltie, and choose a wiser man in his place." He must have particularly disliked mayor Thomas Fowens, whom he called "an insolent fellow," for on one occasion he turned *posteriorem partem corporis sui* toward him and said "scurrilously, contemptuously, rudely and in a high voice," "Come and kisse," and later "I will make thy neck cracke."[1]

Relations grew so strained that in the spring of 1614 Bagge complained to the Privy Council of "divers disgraces and injuries done unto him." The Privy Council wrote to certain Devon magnates to ask them to inquire into the case and mediate it if possible.[2] But their mediation seems to have been useless. The next move was an order by the mayor and some others of the capital burgesses that unless James Bagge "reconcile himselfe to the said Maior and his brethren . . . and withall faithfully promise to demeane himselfe more orderly and temperately for the time to come, that then he shalbe cleane removed from the bench." Bagge made no submission and was accordingly removed. He then sued out a "writ of restitution" in the King's Bench and, the mayor's return being judged insufficient, the court ordered him restored to office.

It is not easy to find the underlying cause of this tempest in a teapot. Bagge was not a mere troublemaker but a substantial citizen. He had himself been mayor and had been commissioned by the national government to do many jobs in connection with the defense of Plymouth and the maintenance of the navy. Besides name-calling and abuse, the mayor's return makes two slightly

1 See the return in *James Bagge's Case*, 11 Co. 93b at 95-97.
2 *Acts of the Privy Council*, 1613-14, p. 411.

more substantial charges against Bagge: (1) The Privy Council by proclamation had forbidden the slaughter of meat during Lent. The mayor of Plymouth then ordered the butchers and innkeepers to put up security that they would comply. Bagge said in public "Master Maior doth more herein than he need, and more than he can well answere," and the butchers and innkeepers consequently refused to give security. (2) He persuaded some of the innkeepers not to make certain customary payments "You need not pay the money for the wine-weight [wine-wyte] any longer except you list, for it is not due unto them." Is there a suggestion here that Bagge was a leader among the innkeepers?

Another possible source of the disagreement may be gathered from Justice Dodderidge's comment on the return, in Rolle's report of the case: "The saying that he wished to avoid the Charter of 43 Eliz. [1601] was no cause to remove him, for it seems to me that such new charters are void, and to me it seems that new Corporations, new Offices and new [blank in the report] will overthrow this Realm, also perhaps this patent [charter] was procured by some persons of the Corporation and the major part never assented to it, and then this would not bind the Corporation . . . some private persons had procured a new Charter for the Town and then the Town refused it."[3] We have mentioned the trend of English boroughs during the sixteenth century toward oligarchy, with self-perpetuating official hierarchies whose members sometimes found their offices very profitable. Justice Dodderidge seems to suggest that James Bagge objected to this development in Plymouth.

3 1 Rol. Rep. 224, 226.

By lawyer's tradition, the writ in this case was the beginning of the modern remedy of mandamus, and in some important respects the tradition is right. There are only two examples of this "writ of restitution" in the printed reports before *James Bagge*. Both are briefly reported by Bulstrode[4] and have since been all but forgotten; but from *Bagge* flowed a continuous stream of legal thought and decision. For all his love of the Year Books, Coke's report of *James Bagge* contains no reference to them (and indeed, hardly any citations to authority at all). Neither seventeenth-century lawyers nor modern scholars have been able to find any cases of mandamus or restitution in the reports or judicial records before 1606 (with arguably one exception which will be discussed below). Nor is there any such writ in the Register of that time.

In the Controlment Rolls of the Court of King's Bench,[5] the writ of restitution as used in *Bagge* can be traced as far as Hilary term, 3 James I (1606), but no further. Eight such writs issued from 1606 to 1615, but in over twenty years before 1606 there are none in the rolls. The two earliest of these writs of restitution are clearly adaptations of existing writs of privilege, used by the central courts to protect their officers and litigants from arrest by the numerous local courts. The one true judicial precedent of an earlier date which was cited as a mandamus in the seventeenth and eighteenth century[6] is also obviously a variation on the notion of privilege, and not on its face a mandamus at all.

4 1 Bulstr. 174 (K.B., Trin. 9 Jac., 1611) and 2 Bulstr. 122 (Trin. 11 Jac., 1613).

5 For a description of the Controlment Rolls, see Appendix A.

6 *Middleton's Case*, Dyer 332b (Common Pleas, Pasch., 16 Eliz., 1574).

The writ in *James Bagge's Case* took the following form, easily seen as a special case of the classical mandamus:

> James, by the grace of God king . . . to the mayor and commonalty of the Borough of Plymouth . . . greeting. Whereas James Bagg was duly chosen and made one of the twelve capital burgesses or magistrates of the said Borough according to the custom used in the aforesaid Borough, and whereas the said James has always behaved and governed himself well in the [said] office . . . You nevertheless, the Mayor and Commonalty of the said Borough, little regarding these premises, did unduly, unjustly and without reasonable cause remove the said James from the office of one of the twelve capital burgesses and magistrates of the said Borough, in contempt of Us and to the no slight damage of the said James and to the injury of his estate, as we have learned from his complaint: We therefore, wishing to do the said James due and prompt justice in this matter, as is just, We order you, and each of you, firmly enjoining you, that immediately on receipt of this writ you shall restore the said James to his aforesaid office of capital burgess and magistrate of the said Borough, with all the liberties, privileges and benefits pertaining thereto, or signify to Us the cause why you do not, lest further complaint come to Us of your default: And show Us how you have executed this writ, three weeks after Trinity, wherever We may then be in England, under penalty of forty pounds, returning to Us then this Our writ. Witness E. Coke at Westminster, 12 June, in the thirteenth year of Our reign.

The earliest writ of restitution in the Controlment Rolls, sued in 1606—not quite ten years before *Bagge*—by one Thomas Tompson against the city of Cambridge, is a very much longer document. It relates with typical medieval verbosity that Tompson had been duly chosen a bailiff of that city and therefore ought to have various fees which pertain to that office. But the mayor, bailiffs, and burgesses of the city

> because of frivolous and private quarrels between you the aforesaid mayor and the said Thomas Tompson . . . deprived, deposed and removed the said Thomas Tompson from the office of bailiff without right or reasonable cause . . . And because the said Thomas Tompson, according to his allegiance to Us and his oath, attempted to exercise his said office further, as it appears, You nevertheless the aforesaid mayor had the same Thomas arrested and detained him in our prison called the Tolbooth *as he was coming to Our court of King's Bench at Westminster last Michaelmas term to confer with his counsel and attorney for the purpose of having their advice in a certain plea of debt by the same Thomas against one Christopher Hutchinson, on demand of sixteen pounds prosecuted in our same court and so far pending undetermined* . . . And the same Thomas has asked us to provide him with an appropriate remedy; We, wishing in this matter to do for the said Thomas that which is just and reasonable, *according to the liberties and privileges of Our aforesaid court* and for Our liege subjects who bring suit therein before Us, that they may prosecute their pleas without indignity, vexation or hindrance, and not wishing to violate or change the ancient customs of the aforesaid city . . . We order you, firmly enjoining you, that if the said Thomas is held by you in the said prison for this reason and no other, then you shall allow the said Thomas to go at large, and you shall restore the said Thomas to his aforesaid office with everything that pertains thereto.[7]

There is no record to show how the *Tompson* case was eventually decided. References to the case in the post-Restoration reports state that he was restored,[8] but this

[7] Controlment Roll (King's Bench), no 246, m. 125 (Hil. 3 Jac., 1605/06). Italics mine.

[8] Rolle's Abridgment (2 Rol. Abr. 456, pl. 4), counsel for the relator

is not probable in view of the state of affairs described in the mayor's return: One of the bailiffs of Cambridge customarily had charge of the borough jail known as the Tolbooth; and every bailiff was required by borough ordinance to put up a bond to save the borough harmless for all charges arising out of his conduct as bailiff. In particular, of course, the prisonkeeper and the borough were liable to the creditor if a man imprisoned for debt escaped, and the bailiffs were expected to give bond against this possibility. Thomas Tompson, shortly after his election as bailiff, took the keys of the Tolbooth from its keeper, Hugh Rose, by force (*violenter eripuit*) and kept them and did what he liked with them for seven days. Hugh Rose, whose position while he did not have the keys was very vulnerable, complained to the mayor, and the mayor three times summoned Tompson to come before the borough council and put up security. Tompson refused to come, saying "I'm busy" (the medieval Latin is even more impudent: "quod ipse habuit alia negocia ad agenda"). Finally, by order of the borough council, he was removed from office and jailed. Thence, he escaped and took his family to Barkway in Hertfordshire.

The important part of the Tompson writ is the italicized passage, for it shows that it is a claim of the privilege of

in *Blagrave's Case* (2 Sid. 49, U.B. Hil. 1657/58), and a footnote in one edition of Dyer's Reports (3 Dyer 332b, Valliant ed., 1794) each state that Tompson was restored because he had been removed without cause. The return shows clearly that there was cause (although arguably not sufficient cause). If all three of these are wrong to such an extent, it is not improbable that they are wrong as to the outcome of the case itself. They may have been misled by a difference of procedure; it would be very natural to mistake the first writ for the alternative writ and the second for the peremptory writ, and in that case the second would have been a judgment for Tompson. But the return to that second writ shows that it was not peremptory and did not result in Tompson's restoration.

the King's Bench. In fact the writ has a general family resemblance to several of the many writs of privilege then in use. For instance, it resembles two *supersedeas pro attornato* in the *Registrum Brevium*, and in the *Thesaurus Brevium* (an unofficial collection supplementing the Register), a *habeas corpus cum causa* and three more *supersedeas*.[9]

Its very close resemblance to two writs of privilege in particular suggests what Tompson's attorney may have had in mind when he (presumably) drafted it. Much of the language seems to be taken from a writ in *Anable's Case* (for the text, see Appendix B), "a precedent before Fortescue, Chief Justice in the time of H[enry] 6," reported only in Dyer's report of *Middleton's Case* (1573).[10] (A similar writ issued in *Middleton* itself, but its text is not reported.) Dyer's report of these cases was published in 1585 and would therefore have been available to Tompson's attorney.

Both Middleton and Anable were freemen of London; each had sued a city official in the central courts at Westminster instead of the local London courts. For his temerity in doing so, each was disfranchised, that is, deprived of his rights as a freeman, and in each case the central court concerned issued a special writ, drawn up for the occasion, ordering restoration of his rights. These two cases do not quite parallel the typical case of privilege, in which a litigant is arrested on his way to or from Westminster. But if the central courts cannot tolerate such arrests, they can still less tolerate that their litigants should be punished for the fact of suing, as in *Middleton;*

9 *Registrum Omnium Brevium Judicialium* (London, 1553); fo. 84, 85 *Thesaurus Brevium* (London, 1687), pp. 134, 298-301.

10 Dyer 332b (Common Pleas, Pasch., 16 Eliz., 1574).

no court can function without power to protect its litigants in this way.

The Tompson writ resembles one used in *Powell v. Aldworth* almost as closely. This was an unpublished action of account in the mayor's court of Bristol, reviewed in King's Bench on writ of error and so preserved in its records. The *Powell* writ ran as follows.

It has been shown to Us on behalf of Richard Powell that whereas he and various of our lieges in coming to Our court of Common Pleas in order to prosecute or defend some suit of writ of debt, remaining there and returning to their own places, ought to be and have used to be under Our protection, according to the liberties and privileges of Our court of Common Pleas used and approved since a time of which no memory remains—A certain person, contriving maliciously to burden heavily the said Richard *as he was coming to Our said court of Common Pleas at this same time for discussion with their counsel and their attorneys to have their advice in a certain plea of debt* on demand of forty pounds sued by one John Boulton against the same Richard . . . in Our said court, in which a writ directed to the same sheriff of the said city is returnable before Our Justices at Westminster five weeks after Easter last past—procured him to be arrested by your subordinates and detained in Our prison in your custody or the custody of some one of you, unjustly, to the same Richard's no slight damage and burden, and contrary to the aforesaid liberties and privileges, Wherefore he has begged Us to furnish him with a remedy, We wishing to do what is right and reasonable for the said Richard and to preserve the liberties and privileges aforesaid inviolably, We order you and each of you, that if the said Richard is detained in Our prison under your custody or the custody of any of you, then you or one of you are to have the same Richard, by whatever name he may be held, along with the day and cause of his taking and detention, before Our Justices at Westminster on the Tuesday next after the octave of Trinity, that the same Justices, having seen the said cause, may do in the matter what ought to be done by right and according to the law and custom of Our realm of England and the liberties and privileges aforesaid. And have there this writ. *Teste* Edmund Anderson, at Westminster, 11 May, 36 Elizabeth.[11]

In this case, Powell's attorney used the writ of privilege in systematic delaying tactics which may have been fairly common at the time. If so, possibly it occurred to Tompson's unknown attorney that the notion of privilege could be used for other tactical maneuvers as well. After issue joined in the Bristol court but before a jury had been impaneled, Powell (the defendant in that court) produced a writ of privilege in the form of a *corpus cum causa ad faciendum et recipiendum* out of the King's Bench. The bailiff of Bristol returned to this writ that Powell had been held for Aldworth's plea of account, that he was now at large on manucaption, and that the plea remained undecided on account of this *corpus cum causa.* Aldworth then produced a writ of procedendo from the King's Bench, and a jury was called. Next, Powell produced the Common Pleas writ which is quoted above, and the Bristol court was again forced to stop its proceedings while it made return to that writ. Aldworth produced another procedendo, on the ground that Powell did not enjoy the privilege of Common Pleas. Lastly, Powell went through the same motions with a habeas corpus ad respondendum from the Exchequer, and it was not until this writ had been duly answered that the Bristol court could proceed to verdict and a large judgment against him, more than twelve years after the suit was originally brought.

11 Coram Rege Roll no. 1390, m. 170 (Pasch., 3 Jac., 1605). Italics mine.

Powell and Tompson each used a variant on the standard claim of privilege, for they were coming to Westminster to confer with their counsel rather than to appear in court. Their claim was probably founded on an entry in Brooke's *Abridgment*: "*Townesend* He who has an attorney and comes to confer with him and is arrested in London shall have the privilege" citing Y.B. 2 Henry 7, fo. 2.[12] In Brooke the statement looks fairly authoritative, but the Yearbook citation describes dinner-table conversation "at Whitefriars" in which Townesend was in a minority of one and relied, moreover, on a case[13] which does not even mention consulting one's attorney. Evidently, however, even such a tenuous claim as this was enough in practice to authorize the issue of the writ. Once issued, a writ of privilege ousted the lower court's jurisdiction automatically, for only the issuing central court could decide whether a party was actually entitled to invoke its privilege.[14]

Although in *Tompson* the King's Bench intervened ostensibly to protect one of its own litigants, an exhausting and fairly exhaustive search of the plea rolls has failed to turn up any trace of *Tompson v. Hutchinson*, the supposed original action of debt in that court. (Since our writ mentions the action as pending in Michaelmas term 1605, the rolls were searched for 1605-1607. It is of course possible that it appears earlier or later in the record.) But if *Tompson v. Hutchinson* was really only part of a maneuver to get Tompson out of the Cambridge jail, it might never be entered on the rolls at all. As soon as Tompson's attorney purchased his writ of debt, he could

12 Sir Robert Brooke, *La Graunde Abridgement* (London, 1586), "*Priviledge*," fo. 154, pl. 34.

13 Y.B. 9 Hen. 6, fo. 7 (Pasch., 1431).

14 *Besome v. Crooke*, Cro. Eliz. 152 (K.B., Mich. 31-32 Eliz., 1589).

have a writ of privilege,[15] but the writ of debt would not be entered in the rolls unless and until the sheriff made his return to it (that he had or had not served it on the defendant).

The law of privilege for litigants in the central courts was very well suited to delaying tactics, as in *Powell v. Aldworth.* For litigants (as distinguished from officers of the court, who could prove their privilege by the record) a jury trial was probably necessary,[16] with all its attendant delays, before a procedendo could issue. The law was, moreover, full of fine factual distinctions offering further scope for delay:

> 1. If a man be arrested coming to the Court at Westminster to answer an action there, he shall have the privilege. . . . 3. If a man is sued in the Bench and he goes to another place by the Court's permission to inquire into evidence in the matter in controversy, he shall have the privilege if he is arrested there. 4. But in such a case if he did not have the Court's permission to go thither, he shall not have the privilege . . . 8. If a man is arrested on his way to London even though he has an action pending in the Bench, yet if he was not coming to that Court, he shall not have the privilege.[17]

15 2 Sir Henry Rolle, *Un Abridgement des Plusieurs Cases et Resolutions del Common Ley* (London, 1668), "Priviledge(C)," 273, citing Y.B. 9 Hen. 6, 54b and other cases. These cases are authority for the proposition that a writ of privilege could issue merely on purchase of an original writ; it is irrelevant for this purpose that later on, after his release from the custody of the lower court, it might be found that he was not entitled to the privilege, for by that time he would be beyond the lower court's reach.

16 *Phips v. Jackson,* 6 Mod. 305 (K.B., Mich., 3 Ann., 1704), is authority that a jury trial was necessary in King's Bench at that date. No earlier case was found on the point; but the length of the delays in *Powell v. Aldworth* tends to support the hypothesis that all three central courts required a jury trial in the early seventeenth century.

17 2 Rolle, *Abridgment,* "Priviledge," 272 (citations omitted).

To summarize this rather involved argument: It seems very likely that Tompson's attorney knew of the writ of privilege as useful for dilatory maneuvers from such cases as *Powell v. Aldworth,* and from these cases he also derived the particular claim of privilege which he made. The notion of using it as a means of restoration to office is a variant on *Middleton* and *Anable,* where the court ordered restoration to a municipal franchise. Much of the language of *Tompson* is also lifted straight from *Anable* and *Middleton.*

Development of the Writ, 1606 to 1615

From *Thomas Tompson* to *James Bagge,* during less than ten years, a most remarkable development of the writ of mandamus may be seen in the record. The new writ changed not only its form but its legal theory almost completely. The change began with *Rex v. London ex rel. Farndon* (1608),[18] a case making use of still another variation on the general idea of privilege.

Edward Farndon was committed to Newgate prison by the mayor and aldermen of London for libeling a clergyman. He then sued out a habeas corpus *ad subjiciendum* in the King's Bench and was released. King's Bench found that before his committal to Newgate he had already been brought before that court and been required to give security for his good behavior. Since then he had behaved well, and had refrained from disturbing the peace in any way; and therefore the cause of detention returned by the London authorities was held to be insufficient in law and invalid. Next, because he had invoked habeas corpus and in disregard of the order of

18 Controlment Roll no. 249, m. 16 (Pasch., 6 Jac., 1608).

King's Bench, the London authorities disfranchised Farndon and ordered his house and shop to be shut and barricaded. Farndon appealed again to King's Bench, and a writ issued ordering him restored to his freedom and his windows and doors opened; this despite the return by the London authorities that Farndon was "a person of exceedingly bad name and fame and degrading conversation, a common barrator, a great disturber of the peace, turbulent, litigious, assiduous in quarrels and strife among his neighbors." The form of the writ (which appears in Appendix B) resembles both *Tompson* and *Anable* very closely.

In all three of these cases King's Bench intervened, in varying circumstances, to protect its litigants from local officials. During the winter following *Farndon* (1608-09), three more writs issued, in a form patterned so closely on *Tompson, Farndon,* and *Anable-Middleton* that the crucial differences in underlying facts almost escapes notice.[19] By this time, it should be noted, there was nearly sufficient authority for an argument that King's Bench can restore to his municipal office or franchise anyone who has been wrongfully removed; and we have seen that there was considerable need for a legal remedy to that end.

In the three cases of 1608-09 the notion of privilege disappeared entirely, and it never returned. The only trace remaining in the writ is an echo of its broad general language. Hereafter, instead of intervening to protect its own litigants, the central court comes in simply "not wishing that Our subjects, because they seek justice in

19 *R. v. St. Albans ex rel. Robinson,* Controlment Roll no. 249 m. 101 (Mich., 6 Jac., 1608); *R. v. Lynn Regis ex rel. Baker, ibid.,* m. 108d (Mich., 6 Jac., 1608); *R. v. Stamford ex rel. Loveday, ibid.,* m. 138d (Hil., 6 Jac., 1608/09).

Our court of King's Bench as it pertains to all Our lieges to do freely and with impunity, should be burdened, vexed or subjected to indignity by anyone" or even more generally "wishing that right and reason should be done to the said Tobias in this matter and not wishing to violate or change the liberties and ancient customs of the said borough, nor that any of our lieges should be unduly burdened or disturbed."[20]

Four years later (Michaelmas term, 10 James, 1612) two more writs of restitution were issued. One of these (*R. v. Lincoln ex rel. Hollingsworth*[21]) follows the verbal pattern of *Tompson* and its immediate successors fairly closely—without mentioning any prior action in King's Bench, or any royal interest in the office, but with all of Tompson's verbosity. The other[22] was intermediate in form. Three more writs[23] issued in the Hilary term following (1612/13). These three are very much shorter and more general

20 *R. v. St. Albans ex rel. Robinson, ibid.*, m. 101 (Mich., 6 Jac., 1608); *R. v. Stamford ex rel. Loveday,* Controlment Roll no. 249 (Hill., 6 Jac., 1608/09). There are suggestions of another legal theory in these early cases, but it seems to be a makeweight and does not survive for long. In the writ for Tompson it is said that the bailiffs of Cambridge, after they have been elected and sworn, "cannot and ought not to be deposed or removed from their office, nor dispensed or relieved of their said oath by anyone but Us and Our successors," apparently because they are sworn "by Us and Our Court." It is probable that this refers to the bailiffs' oath in the borough court; borough courts were commonly described as "curia nostra burgi de ——." As to most municipal offices, the records of disfranchisements and "disalderments" show that they were removeable by majority vote; it must have been common knowledge that the claim that the central court must approve such removals was nonsense. In *Robinson, Loveday,* and *Baker* there is language echoing this theory, but thereafter it all but disappears.

21 Controlment Roll no. 254, m. 78d.

22 *R. v. Lincoln ex rel. Broxholme, ibid.*, m. 78. The writ is set forth in Appendix B.

23 *R. v. Ipswich ex rel. Stewardson, ibid.*, m. 113; *R. v. Liskeard ex rel. Vosper, ibid.*, m. 112d; and *R. v. Lincoln ex rel. Shuttleworth, ibid.*, m. 116. The last is reported in 2 Bulstrode at 122.

in their allegations, and in fact, as this example shows, they cannot be distinguished in form from the writ of *James Bagge:*

> The King . . . to the mayor, sheriff and commons of the city of Lincoln, greetings. Whereas Edmund Shuttleworth, gentleman, was duly elected to the office of first Alderman of the said city of Lincoln according to the custom used in that city, in which office he has governed and carried himself well, You nevertheless, the mayor, sheriff and commons of the said city [a participial phrase illegible] removed the said Edmund from the office of alderman of the said city unjustly, without reasonable cause, in manifest contempt of Us and to the no slight damage and burden of the said Edmund and the hurt of his estate, as we have learned from his complaint. And we, wishing that due and prompt justice should be done the said Edmund in this matter, We order you that immediately on receipt of this writ you restore the said Edmund to his office of Alderman of the said city in his original estate and rank, with all the liberties, privileges and easements pertaining to the said office, lest further complaint should come to us of your default. And you shall cause to appear to us how you have executed this writ wherever we may be in England.

The *Shuttleworth* case is interesting in point of form because in the next term Shuttleworth sued out a new writ (under changed circumstances) which issued in the older, more verbose form.[24] Shuttleworth's failing was carelessness in keeping the town records, "and then sometimes sending a young man his servant, who writes very badly and is very young and ignorant."[25]

Thus by 1613–15 a new writ had appeared with a

24 *R. v. Lincoln ex rel. Shuttleworth,* Controlment Roll no. 255, m. 23 (Pasch., 11 Jac., 1613).

25 *Lincoln Corporation Register* (Historical Manuscript Commission, Report XIV, Appendix, part 8), p. 87.

definite though potentially very flexible form. Moreover, by this writ King's Bench did something quite different from its traditional activities. It was not addressed to the sheriff or any other law enforcement official, like most of the writs in the Register (including habeas corpus and bail). Nor was it directed to other judicial authority like the writs of prohibition, error, *recordari, de cautione admittenda,* and some of the medieval forms of certiorari. By this new writ a public official *outside* the normal law enforcement system was required to do something. Nor yet was this to be done in aid of any of the traditional remedies of King's Bench, like some medieval not-quite-parallels.[26] All this was a very far-reaching departure from tradition. Yet, as may be seen, the writ as it was now worded said nothing to explain why King's Bench could do this, beyond the bare generality that an injustice had been done and it ought to be set right.

Procedure, 1608-1618

The characteristic mandamus procedure of alternative writ, return, and peremptory writ seems to appear in the records soon after *Thomas Tompson. Tompson* itself followed a different course. The first writ stated the case at length, and ended with the mandatory clause: "Vobis mandamus firmiter iniungentes quod si predictus Thomas Tompson ea occasione et non alia in prisona . . . detentus est, tunc ipsum Thomam ad largam ire permittatis quodque predictum Thomam Thompson ad officium suum . . . sine dilacione restituatis."[27] No return day was named

26 For example, *quare non admisit* to a bishop, if he has refused to admit a clerk to a living, on presentation by the patron after the latter has recovered the advowson in question in the secular courts.

27 "We order, firmly enjoining you, that if the aforesaid Thomas Tompson is detained in prison for this reason and no other, then you

and no return entered for this writ. Six months, or two terms, later, another writ issued which is identical with the first except that the corresponding clause begins "Vobis mandamus sicut pluries mandavimus firmiter iniungentes,"[28] and ends with "vel causam nobis significatis quare mandatum nostrum alias vobis inde directum exequi noluistis vel non potuistis,"[29] naming a return day. This is typical of any summons of the period; except that usually there are three steps in the procedure: summons, *alias* (*sicut alias mandavimus*), and *pluries*. The rolls are loaded with *capias*, attachments, and *venires* on this pattern. To the *pluries* a very lengthy return, described above, is entered.

The next case, *R. v. London ex rel. Farndon*, adds a rule to show cause to the summons procedure. After stating Farndon's case, the writ says

> nuper ordinavimus quod nisi causa sufficientis per vos in contrarium inde ostensa esset [day of return] tunc emaneret a curia nostra predicta breve nostrum vobis dirigendum ad restituendum prefatum Edwardum . . . Vosque ad diem illum seu interim aliquam huiusmodi causam in contrarium inde nobis aut curie nostre predicte corum nobis ostendere minime curastis sed omnino neglexistis, Vobis igitur . . . stricte mandamus, firmiter iniungentes quod . . . ipsum Edwardum . . . restituatis . . . Et qualiter hoc preceptum fuerit executum nobis constare faciatis in octabis sancti Hillarii.[30]

---

shall permit the said Thomas to go at large, and that you shall restore the said Thomas to his office without delay."

28 "We order you, as we have many times ordered you, firmly enjoining."

29 "Or show us cause why you did not wish or were unable to execute our command formerly directed to you."

30 "We ordered recently that unless sufficient cause to the contrary should be shown by you [day of return], then our said writ should issue from our court, directing you to restore the said Edward . . . And on

That is, the respondents had entirely ignored a rule to show cause why a writ of restitution should not issue. The next steps in *Farndon* do not appear, for no return was entered in the case. But in *Robinson*,[31] two terms later, the first writ issued included a rule to show cause, like the classical alternative writ. The borough authorities returned that they could not answer this writ because it was directed to the "mayor, bailiffs, and burgesses" of St. Albans, though their proper style was the "mayor and burgesses." Another writ issued immediately on this return, identical in form with the first, except that as in the classical peremptory writ, there was no rule to show cause. Unfortunately there is nothing in the Controlment Rolls to show whether or not this second writ had the effect of a judgment for the relator Robinson (like the classical peremptory writ).

On this evidence a good guess can be made as to the source of two rules of pleading in mandamus. If the writ of restitution was assimilated at first to the various types of summons, it follows that the person on whose behalf the writ issued (he who was later called the relator) was not a party to the proceedings on the return. Those proceedings would concern only the summoning court and the person or persons summoned, although the relator was the real party in interest. From this it follows that the return must be certain, leaving nothing to "intendment" or inference, for the relator "has no day in

that day and since then you have made no effort to show any such cause to the contrary to us or our court, but have totally neglected it, We therefore strictly order you, firmly enjoining you, to restore . . . the said Edward . . . And cause it to be shown to us how this order was executed on the octave of Hilary term." Controlment Roll no. 249, m. 16 (Pasch., 6 Jac., 1608).

31 *R. v. St. Albans ex rel. Robinson*, Controlment Roll no. 249, m. 101 (Mich., 6 Jac., 1608) and m. 137 (Hil., 6 Jac., 1608/09).

court" and cannot elaborate or substantiate it. It follows also that the court is bound to judge by the return, for it has nothing but the writ and the return before it; and therefore if the return is false, the relator has no remedy but an action on the case. Coke states both these rules in *James Bagge's Case*, giving the reason "because the Parties are Strangers, and have no Day in Court,"[32] but without citing any legal authority.

Unfortunately, the records and reports of the earliest cases are too condensed to give much evidence for or against this suggestion. Such evidence as there is tends to support it. In the cases before *James Bagge* the controlment rolls give no indication that the relator was represented, or was not, at the time the returns were made. In the printed reports, the first case in which it appears unambiguously that he was so represented is *R. v. Mayor of Oxford* (ex rel. Harris), in 1627,[33] in which "Littleton moved divers exceptions to the return." The reports before *Harris* seem to be confined to the proceedings on issuing the first writ, the return, and the court's comments on the return; but no reliable inference can be drawn from this fact alone.

Authority for the New Writ

The sudden appearance of such a novel remedy in the Reports, supported only by legal "theory" of such unlawyerlike generality, naturally led to controversy over its legitimacy. Since it was waged by common lawyers, part of this controversy was a search for authority. In each case, the opponent of the writ's issuing could argue (a) there was no authority for restitution (or later, for man-

32 11 Co. at 99b.
33 Palmer 451; Latch 229 (Pasch., 3 Car., 1627).

damus) in this particular case, and (b) there was no authority for restitution or mandamus at all. In fact, it was said, my lord Coke invented the whole thing. In the face of this attack the proponent then had to develop a theory giving the writ greater antiquity and scope. This took the form that the power to issue mandamus derived from the residual power of the King himself to do justice. "Procedents" were cited, many from the Close Rolls of the fourteenth century, to show the antiquity of mandamus. Thus in *S. Balaunce,* Serjeant Noy cites the following picturesque "record made 26 E[dward] 3. in Chancery," that is, in 1352.

> A parish . . . claimed to be of the foundation of King Arthur, and that it was free and exempt from visitation by the bishop; and therefore there was much contention between the bishop and the parson of the parish . . . for which the bishop interdicted them, and would not send them any *Chrisma,* [oil to baptize infants]; upon which they complained and a writ was awarded out of Chancery, and the writ was read to the Court, as follows: Edward, etc., *ex parte* etc., *cum vos* etc. *et vos hoc recusatis,* etc. *Ideo vobis mandamus,* etc.[34]

In *Awdeley v. Joye* the same Serjeant Noy said "that there are precedents to prove this in the times of E. 2, E. 3 and H. 6."[35] In *Dom. Rex v. Mayor of Oxford,* Noy was on the other side, and Littleton (later Chief Justice of the Common Pleas and Lord Chancellor) cites a writ to the mayor and commonalty of Bristol in the sixth year of Edward II. The document referred to is calendared as follows.

[34] Palmer 50.
[35] Popham 176b.

To the mayor and bailiffs and whole community of Bristol. Order, under pain of forfeiture, to restore [names] burgesses of that town to the liberty of the same, from which they have abjudged them and to restore their goods and merchandise to them, according to the king's further order, and to certify the sheriff of Gloucester, whom the king is sending specially to superintend their proceedings in this behalf, of their proceedings. They are to be before the king and his council on a day appointed to answer concerning the above; on which day the king will grievously proceed against them if they refuse to obey this order.[36]

Serjeant William Noy, who was so active in this antiquarian pursuit, was a sad example of the dangers of mixing politics with uncritical historical study. At this date he was still on the popular side of public controversy. In the same year with the case of the mayor of Oxford, Noy represented one of the Five Knights who refused to contribute to a forced loan to the King. In 1628 he argued against Attorney General Heath in the great debate on the liberty of the subject, and afterward proposed a habeas corpus act. When the Lords then proposed that a clause saving the royal prerogative be added to the Petition of Right, Noy opposed it stoutly. Most people were considerably surprised, therefore, when in 1631 he accepted the post of Attorney General. Just before his death in 1634 he suggested ship money as a means of raising funds without calling Parliament—a less than happy idea which was also gleaned from his historial studies.

Some of the fourteenth-century documents thus cited in the seventeenth century are fairly plausible taken in

36 Harvard Law School L MS 2074 (Phillips 7054), fo. 91b; Cal. Close Rolls, 6 Edw. 2, p. 524 (1313).

isolation, as ancestors of mandamus. But all are *ad hoc,* nonjudicial documents drawn up each to fit one particular case, and no connection has ever been shown between them and the activity of the courts in the seventeenth century. Nor, for that matter, has any systematic mandamuslike activity at all been found for the 250 years intervening. Who, then, did invent the new writ?

As has been said, Restoration lawyers who doubted the authenticity of the pre-Stuart precedents for mandamus were inclined to believe that Coke had invented it out of whole cloth. Thus Sir William Jones in Dr. Patrick's great case: "And for authorities, there was no precedent for *Bagge's* case, but the judges finding the mischief, did *out of the foundation of law* frame that writ."[37]

Probably no common lawyer but Coke could have been plausibly suspected of inventing a new writ and a new cause of action outright. He alone had the enormous prestige to carry off such a proceeding; and no one could match his learning to prove him wrong. Yet his opponents knew or at least suspected that he was capable of reading his own views into the old law books. Indeed, as Professor Thorne pointed out in his 1952 Selden Society lecture, "Had he been more fastidious in his use of evidence, or spoken less resoundingly with what Hazlitt and Keats called 'the gusto of the Elizabethan voice' or ever stopped to consider that he might be wrong, he could never have accomplished the impossible task of reconciling the mediaeval and the modern."[38]

The evidence of the Controlment Rolls makes it impossible to believe that Coke personally invented mandamus. It appears in those rolls nearly ten years before

37 T. Raym. 101 at 104 (1665-67). Emphasis mine.

38 S. E. Thorne, *Sir Edward Coke, 1552-1952* (London, 1957), p. 13.

his appointment to the King's Bench; and there is nothing in the record to connect him with the early cases. The writ in *Tompson* is attested by Sir John Popham, then Chief Justice of the King's Bench, and those issued between *Tompson* and *James Bagge*, by Popham's successor, Sir Thomas Flemyng. Since Coke at this time was a justice of the Common Pleas, it is highly unlikely that he had any connection with these cases in any judicial or nonjudicial role.

Somewhat paradoxically, Coke's real contribution to mandamus seems to have been the opposite theory of its historical origin and scope, which he stated in *James Bagge's Case*. The King has power—or rather, once had power—to restore this man to office or to his franchise, because he was unjustly removed and the King can always do justice. This much seems to be assumed. This power the King has delegated to his Court of King's Bench; he cannot now exercise it personally because in some sense this case is *propria causa regis*, and no man can be judge in his own cause. Even more important was Coke's view of the scope of this power. It extends to "errors and misdemeanors extra-judicial, tending to the breach of the peace, or oppression of the subjects, or raising of a faction, controversy or debate, or to any other manner of misgovernment; so that no wrong or injury either public or private, can be done, but that this shall be reformed or punished by due course of law."[39] Other examples of this general jurisdiction to do justice are the powers to grant habeas corpus, prohibition, and bail as against all inferior courts.

This sweeping claim of power was of course one

39 11 Co. at 98.

manifestation of Coke's central belief, as a judge, in the supremacy of the common law. For his great Bractonian slogan "The King ought not to be under any man, but under God and the law," which King James said "is treason to affirm,"[40] is implicit in the phrase "any manner of misgovernment" (as the author of the *Observations on the Lord Coke's Reports* points out[41]). In some measure *Bagge's Case* probably contributed to Coke's downfall; and afterward this paragraph was singled out by Bacon and Ellesmere as one of the five unforgivable errors in Coke's reports.[42]

So controversial a theory might well have died at birth; and it may be that the growth of mandamus as a broader remedy than the writ of restitution was hindered by its political baptism. Yet it began to grow very soon, and in a sense its ultimate scope was nearly as broad as Coke's language.

Coke said that at one time or another the King had delegated all of his judicial power to the courts: "the King hath committed all his power judicial, some to one court, some to another, so as if any would render himself to the

40 12 Co. 65.

41 "He doth as much as insinuate that this court [the King's Bench] is all sufficient in itself to manage the state; for if the King's Bench may reform any manner of misgovernment (as the words are) it seemeth that there is little or no use, either of the King's royal care and authority exercised in his person and by his proclamations, ordinances and immediate directions, nor of the Council Table, which under the King is the chief watch tower for all points of government, nor of the Star Chamber, which hath ever been esteemed the highest court for extinguishment of all riots and public disorders and enormities; and besides the words do import as if the King's Bench had a superintendency over the government itself, and to judge wherein any of them do misgovern." Pages 11-12, quoted in 5 W. E. Holdsworth, *History of English Law* (London, 1938), 430, n. 3. The *Observations* are attributed to Lord Ellesmere, but there is little evidence that they were his.

42 5 Holdsworth, *H.E.L.*, 478, n. 1.

judgment of the King in such case where the King hath committed all his power judicial to others, such a render should be to no effect."[43]

If there was such a delegation or series of delegations, the process must have been completed before the time of Henry IV, for Coke cites cases from that reign to show that the delegation has been made. The documents cited by the proponents of restitution were chiefly of the mid-fourteenth century, from which it might be inferred that the supposed delegation took place sometime in the last third or quarter of the fourteenth century. But if this was the case, it is remarkable that the courts seem never to have exercised that power from 1400 to 1606. There are no cases in the black-letter Year Books, nor in the printed law reports before Coke, that can fairly be called mandamus or restitution. Nor are there any such cases in the Controlment Rolls of King's Bench in the years 1584-1605, although as we have seen, there were a significant number in the years 1606-1615.

It is perhaps hardly fair to expect close critical analysis of documents from Coke or any other seventeenth-century legal historian. But his argument is not sufficient even in logic to account for the exercise of this power by King's Bench. He argues that the King must have delegated his judicial power in these cases, because they are *propriae causae regis*, and he cannot be judge in his own cause. If there is a hidden circularity in this argument—for a habeas corpus or a writ of restitution is the king's own cause only formally, because the King's Bench has jurisdiction over it, and not in the sense that the King is an interested party—Coke failed to see it. Nor on its

43 Sir Edward Coke, *The Fourth Part of the Institutes of the Laws of England* (London, 1648), at 71.

face does the argument give any reason why King's Bench should have this power and not some other court. Coke's conscious purpose, of course, was to argue that King James personally did not have it.

As we have shown, *James Bagge* is singularly unsupported by authority, for the simple reason that there was no authority except in the most recent records of the Court. Coke refers only to the general language of Magna Carta, c. 29b, "No free man shall be disseised . . . of his liberties or customs . . . unless by the judgment of his peers or the law of the land"; he was unable to give any less general authority for this exercise of judicial power.

Out of *James Bagge* and Coke's sweeping theory came a development in the next one hundred and fifty years whose end product was the writ of mandamus as we know it. The obvious usefulness and moral appeal of Coke's doctrine in many cases, with the prestige of its great proponent, weighed in its favor. Against it were its startling scope and complete lack of any other authoritative support at the beginning. In the next one hundred and fifty years, on the one hand, the use of mandamus was gradually extended in varying fact situations; and on the other, lawyers and judges sought for limitations appropriate to so broad a theory. In the end, the scope of the original writ of restitution was extended to nearly "any manner of misgovernment" in a substantive sense; but procedural and other limitations were found to preserve the proper freedom of action of government officials and the structure of the common law.

At a much later period than Coke seems to have had in mind, the royal prerogative may have made a contribution to the new remedy. The Privy Council of Queen Elizabeth I often intervened in municipal affairs. In fact it appears that whenever a dispute over borough or city politics became bitter—and as we have seen the sixteenth century was a period of change and controversy—one side or the other was likely to call in the Council. Thus about 1590 the Corporation of Doncaster petitioned the Privy Council to settle a dispute about the election of the mayor. The existing mayor, aldermen, and common council, who together constituted the corporation of the town, claimed the right to elect the next mayor according to "continued usage and custom not heretofore called in question." The commonalty of the town claimed the same right by the words of the borough charter, and elected a different candidate. The Privy Council referred the dispute to Justices Clinche and Walmesley for their opinion as to the proper mode of election. The justices found for the corporation on the basis of custom, and the Privy Council made an order accordingly.[44]

In such cases the Council made a practice of referring the dispute to some other group to hear the evidence and make recommendations for a settlement. Sometimes this was an *ad hoc* group of gentlemen or high church dignitaries; in appropriate cases it might be the Council for Wales or for the North; and sometimes, as in the example above, it was a group of Her Majesty's justices. I have not seen evidence that the judges were employed often enough to give them any real experience in dealing with these problems, let alone often enough for them to develop a body of law. Nevertheless some publicity was given to the problems and some experience did result. Unfortunately we cannot trace whether there was any closer connection than this between the Council's activity

[44] *Acts of the Privy Council,* 1590-91, pp. 19, 86; 1591, pp. 128, 261 (5 Oct. 1590 to 5 July 1591).

and the new writ, because a fire at Whitehall in 1618 burned all the Council's records for the crucial period 1601-1613. James Bagge himself appealed to the Privy Council in 1614,[45] but although the Council named mediators they did not settle the case.

It is clear that the Privy Council's approach to these cases was quite different from that of the courts later on. The Council came in as mediator rather than judge, with a primary interest in keeping the peace and therefore in settling the whole controversy, rather than in doing justice to a petitioner who claimed to have been disfranchised unjustly. And although the records suggest the beginnings of a systematic procedure for dealings with these cases, the Council cannot fairly be said to have "exercised a jurisdiction" over them which was later passed on to the Courts of King's Bench.

From the speed with which the writ of restitution took shape once the potentialities of the law of privilege in these cases were understood, as well as from the frequency with which the new writ was used, it appears that such a remedy must have been much wanted. The question is then why so many people should claim to have been unjustly removed from office. As we have seen, both disfranchisement and "disalderment" were very common measures at that time. They were used both as punishments for infractions of bylaws and as political weapons; indeed, in the sixteenth and early seventeenth centuries there was little distinction between misconduct and legitimate disagreement with authority.

There was no single pattern for the political disputes of the time, although the use of borough lands and the powers of the commonalty and the common council, as in

45 *Acts of the Privy Council*, 1613-14, p. 411.

Doncaster, are themes that recur fairly often. There were three pre-*Bagge* cases which came up from the City of Lincoln in 1612. William Broxholme was disfranchised becaused he disputed the city's title to part of its common lands.[46] Leon Hollingsworth defied the authority of the mayor and aldermen in various ways, including "vile and despiteful speeches which cannot for modesty be recited" and "outrageous railings" in meetings. Since Hollingsworth had himself been mayor, and was later reconciled to the then mayor and aldermen, we may take it that his grievance was probably political.[47] Edmund Shuttleworth was displaced as Town Clerk for neglect of his duties, carelessness in keeping records, and absence from the city.[48] In Chester in 1574 a number of persons were disfranchised during a controversy over the jurisdiction of the Court of Exchequer there.[49] At Stamford there was a dispute, apparently over the spending of the borough revenues, which lasted from March 1588/89 to 1592 and perhaps flared up again in later years.[50] A burgess of Devizes was disfranchised for allowing visitors from a plague-infected area to stay with him, contrary to a borough ordinance.[51] Persistent drunkenness, non-residence (so as to avoid borough taxes while keeping the valuable right to trade in the borough), and contempt of the mayor are other common causes for disfranchisement.

By the time of *James Bagge's Case* the new writ of

46 *Lincoln Corporation Register*, pp. 88, 90, 91.

47 *Ibid.*, pp. 88, 89.

48 *Ibid.*, pp. 85, 87.

49 *Acts of the Privy Council*, 1571-75, pp. 223-228.

50 *Acts of the Privy Council*, 1588-89, pp. 91, 224, 232, 262; 1589-90, pp. 124, 368; 1591-92, p. 447; 1599-1600, p. 73.

51 B. Howard Cunnington, *Some Annals of the Borough of Devizes, 1555-1791* (Devizes, 1925), part II, p. 37.

restitution had not a shred of legal theory to support or explain it. It had completely lost any connection with the writ of privilege, without as yet acquiring any more general theoretical basis. When Bagge's alternative writ was awarded the court said only "that one Baker of Lynn was restored here on such a writ, and this course is usual."[52] The same lack of theoretical underpinning appears in the cautious reasoning of *Shuttleworth v. City of Lincoln* two years earlier. Edmund Shuttleworth had been elected alderman in place of another man who had been removed for cause, but he was in turn ousted when his predecessor was restored by writ from King's Bench. On his application for restitution when next there was a vacancy, the Court said "that they could not write to them to elect such a one, *this Court being only to deal in cases of Restitution . . . upon bad and undue removalls.*"[53]

Mandamus and Freehold

With Lord Coke's report of *James Bagge*, first published in 1616, possible theories for the new writ began to develop. One was the magniloquent theory favored by Coke himself, who, as we have seen, saw in King's Bench, "Authority, not only to correct Errors in judicial Proceedings," but nearly all "Errors and Misdemeanors extrajudicial." Although to the legal mind this conception was so spacious and incapable of precision as to be almost nonexistent, it had a persistent moral appeal, engendering some fine broad language in the cases of the next fifty years. Thus in *Awdeley v. Joye*[54] it was said: "This Court hath power not only in judiciall things, but also in some

52 1 Rol. Rep. 173 (Pasch., 13 Jac., 1615).
53 2 Bulstr. 122 (Trin., 11 Jac., 1613). Italics mine.
54 Popham 176b (Pasch., 2 Car., 1626).

things which are extrajudicial . . . and this thing is peculiar to this Court, and is one of the flowers of it . . . And it was said by the Justices that they are the chief conservators of the Peace within the Realm, and therefore have power for the preservation of the Peace in such factious Towns to grant restitution." In Sir Thomas Raymond's report of the great case of *Dr. Patrick*, it will be remembered, counsel argued that the writ had been framed "out of the foundation of law."[55]

A second theory suggested by Coke treated the new writ as a consequence of Magna Carta, c. 29.[56] From this provision of the charter the inference seems to have been drawn that restitution would lie when and only when a subject was wrongfully disseised of a freehold. The underlying assumption of the cases seems to be that any office may be held in freehold if it is an office of profit and held in fee or for life,[57] but there is little case law on the point except for offices granted by royal letters patent. In particular I have found no authority outside the mandamus cases holding that a municipal alderman had a freehold in his office. He did hold for life unless removed for cause, or unless the city charter specified otherwise.

55 T. Raym. 101 at 104 (Hil., 16 & 17 Car. 2, 1664/65).

56 In Coke's report the charter is cited only as the reason why "the Cause of his Disfranchisement ought to be an Act or Deed, and not a Conation or an Endeavor." 11 Co., Rep. at 98b. But in 1 Rol. Rep. at 225, Coke is quoted as giving the charter a much broader application. "Coke to the same intent, we are now in our proper element, namely to reform abuses in manners on such a writ as this is as good as reforming errors; this Bagg was one of the Privy council of the Town, and was a partaker of the liberties there, and had in a manner an inheritance in them, and the statute of Magna Carta is that nullus liber homo disseisetur de libertatibus ou consuetudinibus nisi per pares vel legem terre, and in this case Bagg was not disfranchised and ousted from his liberties per pares, that is, by a jury, nor per legem terre."

57 *Jehu Webb's Case*, 8 Co. 45b at 47 (Mich., 6 Jac., 1608), and 2 Coke, *Inst.* 412 (discussing the statute of Westminster II, c. 25).

Coke's capacity for creative generalization appears to have been at work here as elsewhere.

A simple theory of freehold had some currency in the seventeenth century. Thus in *Warren's Case*[58] it was held that although an alderman, having a freehold in his office, could not be removed without cause, and a custom allowing such removal was void, nevertheless a member of the common council could be so removed by custom, because the common council is "a thing collateral to a corporation." In *Awdeley v. Joye* the question was whether restitution would lie for one who held only a grant of the office in reversion, "expectant upon an Estate for life," and so was never seised. The notion that restitution is essentially a remedy for an injury to property of a certain kind appears more definitely in *R. v. Mayor of Oxford* in which counsel for the city argues that Alderman Harris cannot be restored "in that it is a place of burden and not of profit . . . [and] the writ of restitution does not mention that he has any benefit from being Alderman nor loss by not being one."[59] The decision in the case is not reported. Twenty years later Serjeant Glynn, recorder of London and later Chief Justice of the Upper Bench during the Commonwealth, argues that "the very nature of the Writ of Restitution . . . is to restore the party to a freehold or some other matter of profit . . . and a writ of Restitution is to restore one to a possession, where one may not be restored in an ordinary way."[60] In *Isle's Case* in 1671,[61] mandamus was first denied to restore a sexton and then

58 Cro. Jac. 540 (Trin., 17 Jac., 1619).

59 Latch 229, Palmer 451 (Pasch., 3 Car., 1627). Harris had not been disfranchised, which would in itself have meant the loss of valuable trading privileges.

60 *Estwick v. City of London*, Style 32, 42 (Trin., 23 Car., 1647).

61 2 Keb. 802, 807, 820.

later granted on a showing that this particular sexton was elected by the parish for his lifetime, and received twopence from each parishioner per annum. Restitution was denied to one of the "Approved Men of Guildford" because he had only been suspended from office and so no freehold was involved.[62]

But the freehold theory alone, though it found adherents for many years, was an inadequate formula for what the court was doing from the first. Restitution was granted for several nonfreehold offices, as a churchwarden who is elected annually at Easter time,[63] and it was agreed that it would lie for a constable, also elected annually.[64] Chief Justice Glynn suggested another theory in the *Case of the Clerk of the City Works*, saying that mandamus would lie, even though the office was not sworn: "1. To restore one to an office which concerns the exercise of justice. 2. If the office or degree is for the public weal."[65]

Nor would mandamus lie for every freehold interest in Coke's sense. In *Middleton's Case*, the question was whether mandamus would lie to restore one to the treasurership of a waterworks company, "which was much opposed by Coleman and Powys, because it was only a thing of private concernment, and not touching the publick." "And at the last the Court granted the [alternative] mandamus in this case, and said that they will hear

62 1 Keb. 868 (Pasch., 17 Car. 2, 1665).

63 *Case of the Parish of S. Balaunce*, Palmer 50 (Mich., 17 Jac., 1619). From an unpublished MS of the case in the Harvard Law School Library, and from the records, it appears that the place name is properly Sutton Valence.

64 1 Bulstr. 174 (Trin., 9 Jac., 1611).

65 2 Sid. 112 (Mich., 1658). There seems to have been a tentative theory that mandamus would lie to every office to which one was sworn: this would cover the churchwarden and the constable. But I have seen no other suggestion of it in the cases after about 1610.

argument whether it lay on the return. But it was agreed by all that mandamus lies to restore the steward of a court leet, because his place deals with the administration of justice. But it does not lie to restore the steward of a court baron to his place, because it is private."[66] In *Daniel Appleford's Case*[67] (one of the group of college cases discussed below), counsel for the respondent New College, Oxford, says:

I conceive that this is such a college as no *mandamus* should go to it in any case whatsoever; for it is but a private society, and hath no influence upon the public . . . and there were no judicial *mandamus's* till Bagge's Case; and I never knew them go but when the party had not only a freehold, but one that was of public concern; now a fellowship of a college is for a private design only to study.

New Uses for the Writ

By this time, however, the court's activity had gone beyond the restitution formula itself. Strictly speaking, this growth began as early as 1619, for in the *Case of the Parish of S. Balaunce*,[68] the question was not restoration to an office previously held but admission to it when duly elected. An interesting case of the same year makes the same broader application of the writ, and shows also the underlying sense of legality in general out of which the true mandamus eventually developed.

The Portreeve of Evill [Yeovil] in the County of Somerset had always been used to be elected to continue in his office for a year . . . and to be sworn in the Leet by the steward of Sir Edward Phillips, lord of the manor; which was refused to be

66 1 Sid. 169, 1 Lev. 123 (Mich., 15 Car. 2, 1663).
67 1 Mod. 82 at 83, Hil., 23 and 24 Car. 2 (1671/72).
68 Palmer 50 (Mich., 17 Jac., 1619).

done on account of discord with Sir Edward Phillips; for which process was awarded out of the King's Bench on motion of Serjeant Ashley, commanding the oath to be tendered to the Portreeve, for the Court of King's Bench is the Supreme Court, which must do justice to all the King's subjects.

[A little later] The justices now on the view of a record 34 E.I. that the Portreeve of Evill had taken an oath in the court of the Lord of the Manor of Evill to make suit and services in the Court of the said Lord, and to collect his rents as his bailiff, the judges refused to enjoin Sir Robert [*sic*] Phillips the lord of the said manor to administer any other oath than the said old oath.[69]

A more radical departure from the restitution context begins with the unpublished case of *R. v. Mayor and Aldermen of London ex rel. Crispe.*[70] The writ in this case orders the mayor and aldermen to give judgment in a case before them in their judicial capacity. The mayor and aldermen made a return to the writ, but the final result of the proceedings does not appear. A very significant new use of the writ was made in *Luskins v. Carver*,[71] where it was awarded to command the Prerogative (ecclesiastical) Court to appoint the executor named by the deceased in his will. The name "mandamus" appears for the first time in this case. After these decisions comes a series of nonrestitution mandamuses to compel the officials of a London parish to carry out their duty to appoint scavengers;[72] to compel the spiritual court to appoint the next-of-kin as administrator when the executor named in the will has refused to serve;[73] to compel a sheriff who

69 *Portreeve of Evill's Case*, 2 Rol. Rep. 82, 85, Pasch., 17 Jac. (1619).
70 Controlment Roll no. 275, m. 118, Hil., 2 Car. (1626/27).
71 Style 7, Mich., 22 Car. (1646).
72 *Anon.*, Style 346, Mich. 1652.
73 *Anon.*, 2 Sid. 114, Mich. 1658.

has been (lawfully) removed to deliver the records of the office to his successor;[74] to a mayor, to compel him to enroll one who has finished his apprenticeship as a freeman of the city;[75] to require a municipal court to enter judgment, where the verdict has gone for the relator.[76]

A more comprehensive theory of mandamus developed as the writ grew beyond the formula of restitution to office. It began as an analogy to the ancient writ of prohibition—first drawn in the cases so early as 1619, in *S. Balaunce*. Some key conceptions of the law of mandamus, in particular the relationship between "keeping inferior courts in their jurisdiction" and "putting the laws into execution," have their origin in this analogy, and therefore some review of the law of prohibition and some general discussion of these ideas will be necessary before considering the later developments in mandamus. But because these ideas are also important for certiorari "to quash," the second of our two new remedies, it will be convenient to discuss the origins of that writ at this point.

74 *Case of the Sheriff of Nottingham*, 1 Sid. 31, Hil., 12 & 13 Car. 2 (1660/61).

75 *Townsend's Case*, T. Raym. 69 (Hil., 14 & 15 Car. 2, 1662/63).

76 *Amherst's Case*, T. Raym. 214 (Hil., 23 & 24 Car. 2, 1671/72).

III

CERTIORARI: ORIGINS

THE USE of the writ of certiorari "to quash," that is, to review orders of a more or less administrative nature, does not begin to appear in the printed cases until the year 1642. More will be said below of *Commins v. Massam*,[1] the very remarkable first reported case of this type, after we have attempted to trace the beginnings of the new legal form and the new remedy.

Unlike mandamus, certiorari is a comparatively slight adaptation of a much older formula. The generic writ certiorari made its first appearance early in the 1270's, just before Edward I came to the throne: it is impossible to be wholly precise about the date because the case materials in print are few and severely edited.[2] Also, the date of its first appearance is partly a matter of somewhat arbitrary definition.

CERTIORARI IN THE MIDDLE AGES

The medieval certiorari was a by-product in the development of the writ of error during the thirteenth and

1 March 196 (Pasch., 18 Car., 1642).

2 Since this question is peripheral to this study, it was not given a high priority during the time spent in the Public Record Office. Part of the answer is undoubtedly there.

early fourteenth centuries. An undifferentiated certiorari form appears first in the rolls, but in the beginning this form was used very largely to correct errors in the lower courts. Early in the fourteenth century the characteristic language of error was added to certiorari, making the writ of error; and thereafter the older form was used only for miscellaneous other purposes.

Parts of the language of certiorari and error derive from the much older writs of false judgment, namely *recordari facias* and *accedas ad curiam*.[3] These were writs by which a "record" was made up for a court not technically of record, and was sent to Westminster to be re-examined. *Recordari* lay to the county courts, *accedas ad curiam* to courts baron. In early times this "record" was reported orally by four knights, suitors of the inferior court, who had been present when the judgment in question was given. Indeed, in Glanville's time the knights might be required to defend that judgment by battle.[4]

During the thirteenth century written statements instead of an oral report began to be required in these proceedings against courts not of record.[5] At the same time a procedure for correcting errors against courts of record was developed, whose origins must now be considered.

Since the Assize of Northampton, 1176, justices in eyre

[3] For the texts of these writs, see Appendix C.

[4] 1 Holdsworth, *H.E.L.*, 73, n. 7.

[5] For details of this process and of the general development of the writ of error see S. F. C. Milsom's "The Origins and Early History of Judicial Review in England," (unpubl. diss., University of Cambridge, 1957). He points out that in the earliest proceedings of this type the "appellant's" main purpose was to punish an unjust judge, and reversal of the judgment was only incidental. Thus the proceeding was actually "against" the court below.

had been required to report any case "so great that it cannot be decided without the lord King, or the like" to the king or "those who shall be in his place" for their consideration.[6] Also, according to the chronicle of Benedict the Abbot of Peterborough[7] when the Common Bench was established difficult cases were ordered to be reserved for the King and his "wiser men." Historians do not agree on how or by whom these difficult cases were removed nor on who reviewed them: indeed, it seems probable on the face of it that different methods were tried out at different times in the hundred years following. During the reign of Henry III difficult matters were generally reserved for the King's council, but at an earlier time they were probably simply adjourned until a day when the king or his justiciar would be present in the court, or until justices in eyre could consult him.[8]

S. F. C. Milsom believes that true proceedings in error came into being shortly after A.D. 1215, because of Magna Carta's requirement that the possessory assizes be heard in the counties rather than at Westminster.[9] The administrative problem posed by this requirement was met by empowering ordinary knights of the shires to take assizes. These knights were not particularly learned in the law, nor was the central government especially anxious to protect their dignity. They were the same men whose judgment, as suitors of the county court, could be questioned by writ of false judgment, and it must have seemed very natural to review their judgments as commissioners of assizes also. As Milsom says, the writs for this purpose

6 Assize of Northampton, c. 7, printed in Stubbs, *Select Charters Illustrative of English Constitutional History* (Oxford, 1913), at 180.

7 I, 207, excerpted in Stubbs, *Select Charters*, at 155.

8 Milsom, "Origins of Judicial Review," pp. 126f.

9 Magna Carta, c. 18; Milsom, "Origins of Judicial Review," pp. 136f.

were probably not fixed in form during most of the reign of Henry III, but were drawn up specially for each case. It is possible, however, that examination of the plea rolls for the years 1250-1272 would show that a definite form of the writ did appear; the printed cases give no conclusive answer on this point.[10]

In the last year of the reign of Henry III the phrase *certis de causis* or *quibusdam certis de causis*, the distinguishing feature of certiorari in classical common-law jurisprudence, made its first appearance.[11] Thereafter it is quite common in the records of King's Bench (as edited by G. O. Sayles and published by the Selden Society[12]) as well as in the *Abbreviatio Placitorum*. There are twenty-seven cases in Sayles's first volume in which the writ is clearly certiorari: Eighteen of these were sent up for the purpose of reviewing errors after judgment. In some of these cases the plaintiffs "dicunt quod erratum est,"[13] and in a few the writ is paraphrased "rex . . . certiorari et errorem si quis intervenit corrigi volens."[14]

One of the four cases in Sayles in which certiorari was used for an interlocutory appeal may serve to illustrate the gradual development of the writ of error. Ralph de

10 There is one case in the *Abbreviatio Placitorum—Adam de Stratton v. Richard of Lincoln*, p. 182 (1272)—in which the writ appears to be recited in indirect speech and to contain a statement of its special circumstances set out in detail. The same is true of a number of entries in the Close Rolls: Calendar, 1251-53, pp. 223, 445; 1254-56, p. 154; 1261-64, pp. 224, 301; 1268-72, pp. 531, 525. These entries more and more approximate the classic certiorari.

11 *William son of Simon v. William Belet*, Abbr. Plac., p. 184 (1272).

12 G. O. Sayles, ed., *Select Cases in the Court of King's Bench under Edward I* (London, 1936-1939), 3 volumes, *passim*.

13 "Say that there was error." For example, 2 Sayles, *King's Bench* at 44, 45 at 48 (1291).

14 "The king . . . wishing to be informed and that error should be corrected if any has occurred." For example 1 Sayles, *King's Bench*, 168 (1287).

Cuylly demanded the manor of Edston of the abbot of Bec-Hellouin in Normandy (then a large landholder in England; its name survives in the London suburb of Tooting Bec). The suit was adjourned from day to day in the Common Bench for lack of knights to take the grand assize. Before the day to which it had been adjourned, the abbot had the record removed into King's Bench, apparently on certiorari.

And the attorney of the aforesaid abbot . . . asked what the grievances are of which he complains, says that he is aggrieved in other matters than those which are recorded by the roll of the aforesaid justices. For he says that on the Octave of Hilary, when he had come forward against the aforesaid Ralph on the aforesaid plea, and the aforesaid Ralph had many times been called for, he appeared neither by himself nor by an attorney; but at length a certain man brought himself forward, making himself the attorney of the aforesaid Ralph. And he challenged him as not being his attorney and definitely put himself on the default, to the gain or loss of the whole suit . . . Wherefore he now asks, as then he asked, that the default which the aforesaid Ralph made on that day should be allowed him. And because nothing is found in the aforesaid record about the said challenge, enquiry is made of the aforesaid justices . . . They say that indeed . . . on the aforesaid day . . . a certain man appeared who made himself the aforesaid Ralph's attorney, and the abbot's aforesaid attorney immediately challenged him as a false attorney . . . enquiry was made of him concerning his name, and he called himself Richard of Newton; and the abbot's aforesaid attorney, on hearing that name, challenged him the more, wherefore the clerks were ordered to scrutinize the rolls of the attorneys . . . And so that no substitution could be made of one person for another, the aforesaid attorney, so challenged, was made to stand upright on the table where the clerks place their rolls, so that his person could be definitely known at another time. Afterwards . . . the rolls of attorneys were searched and in them it was found that the aforesaid Ralph made one Nicholas of Upton his attorney. And when this was known, the attorney of the aforesaid abbot betook himself definitely to the default of the said Ralph to the gain and loss of the whole plea, on this ground, that on the preceding day the aforesaid Ralph did not appear by himself or by any attorney called Nicholas of Upton, but rather by a man who called himself Richard of Newton. And the aforesaid attorney who was challenged said that he was the Nicholas of Upton who was found in the roll of attorneys. And . . . when he called himself Richard of Newton he was out of his senses and did not know what he said, and he asks that his lack of experience should not prejudice his lord, but offered to prove by the country [i.e., by jury] . . . that he is called Nicholas of Upton . . . And . . . it seemed to them [the justices of the Common Bench] that it would be hard and unjust if the aforesaid Ralph should incur disinheritance through the silliness of his attorney, who witlessly made a mistake in his own name, and they gave a day for four knights to come [to proceed with the assize.]

But King's Bench gave judgment to the abbot, because "it is not customary that those things which are avowed and confessed in the king's court should receive proof to the contrary by the country" and the challenged attorney could not otherwise prove that he was Nicholas of Upton. On the record, therefore, Ralph had defaulted.[15] The interest of the case lies in the fact that King's Bench, in this sort of early quasi-error proceeding, had already recognized a problem in errors not "on the face of the record." Within less than ten years it had become clear that only errors "on the face" would be reviewed, and Chapter 31 of the Statute of Westminster II had been

15 1 Sayles, *King's Bench*, 16 (1275).

enacted (1285), over judicial opposition, providing for bills of exceptions to bring up errors not "on the face." That is, questions of "scope of review" and the "face of the record" rule had arisen even before the writ of error was clearly distinguished from certiorari. They reappeared in the seventeenth-century growth of certiorari, and have caused trouble down to our own day.

In two of the cases printed by Professor Sayles in his first volume, certiorari was used to attack an indictment (before trial) as erroneous or insufficient; this remained as one of the classical uses of certiorari. In two cases the writ was used to begin interlocutory appeal proceedings, and in five the record was called up for a purpose not strictly appellate or not appellate at all.

The specific writ of error, beginning "Quia in recordo et processu, ac etiam in redditione judicii . . . error intervenit manifestus"[16] was first used against royal justices sometime between 1300-1320. Professor Milsom has found a model for it in a writ to the local courts of London, contained in a Register of Writs[17] assigned to the first half of Edward I's reign (about 1272-1290). At this point certiorari ceased to be used to correct final judgments, where the writ of error would lie, but it continued to be used in numerous other situations where a record of any kind was wanted.

To examine or even to list all the medieval forms and uses of certiorari would require a lengthy digression from the main purpose of this discussion. For many judicial and administrative purposes, as Professor Plucknett says, it was the medieval equivalent of "Get me the file on

16 "Because in the record and process, and also in the judgment given . . . manifest error has occurred."

17 Harvard Law School MS 52 (unfoliated).

such and such a matter." It seems that a judge of the central court could call up any matter of judicial or administrative record which became relevant to a pending legal action. Sometimes, as in attaint of a jury or debt on a record, the record of an earlier lawsuit was the essence of the controversy, and certiorari was the writ used to bring it before the court.

The Register of Writs of 1553 contains many other such certioraris, as for instance: A writ to the sheriff commanding him to certify "whether he who has the king's protection (a special document) has set forth on the king's business or not." If he had done so, a supersedeas would issue to stay most suits against him, but if not there would be a procedendo to proceed with the suit.[18] On a writ of right the tenant might plead that the land in question was of the ancient demesne and so not liable to action by writ of right. A certiorari would then issue to the Lord Treasurer and Chamberlain to look it up in Domesday Book; similarly when the question was by what services a particular manor was held.[19] When a clerk was presented to a church, prohibition would issue to the appropriate bishop on suggestion that an action *quod permittat* was pending in the Bench concerning the advowson of this church. The opposing claimant (apparently) could then have certiorari to the justices of the bench for the record and process of this *quod permittat*, and if they returned that no such action was pending, a writ would issue to the bishop to proceed.[20] At folio 209 of the *Register* are a very large group of certioraris for use in connection with the possessory assizes for land.

18 *Reg. Brevium* (1553), fo. 24, 24b, and fo. 220 for the procedendo.
19 *Ibid.*, fo. 14b.
20 *Ibid.*, fo. 31b, certiorari and the following *breve inde episcopo*.

Certiorari was used in early times to send up the record when a man convicted of homicide *se defendendo* sought the royal pardon, to which he was entitled in the regular course[21]—a procedure which seems to have become obsolete during the reign of Edward III. Similarly it was used in connection with the royal pardon for outlawry, when the defendant in a civil suit had suffered judgment by default and execution against him had gone to the point of outlawry.[22]

The use of certiorari to remove cases from "base courts" into King's Bench for trial requires somewhat more detailed discussion. Certiorari lay to courts of record for this purpose. For base courts not of record (franchise courts, borough courts, communal courts) and for the courts of counties palatine even though they were courts of record the appropriate writ was *recordari facias.*[23] Thus certiorari was commonly used to remove indictments from before justices of peace,[24] sometimes for presentments before commissioners of sewers,[25] occasionally for cases in the sheriff's turn.[26] In medieval times the certiorari issued from the Chancery and the return was made "before Us in Our Chancery," the record being then sent on to the King's Bench by writ of mittimus.[27] But at least by the end of the sixteenth century King's Bench

21 *Ibid.*, fo. 286b; 26 Ass. Pl., pleas 23 and 32, cited in 3 Holdsworth, *H.E.L.*, 312, n. 3.

22 *Reg. Brevium* (1553), fo. 283b.

23 1 Brooke, *Abridgement*, fo. 117b, pl. 36 and fo. 116b, pl. 5 (title *Cause a remover plee*) citing Y.B. 9 Hen. 6 [fo.] 58.

24 Y.B. Trin. 12 Hen. 7, pl. 3, fo. 25 (1496).

25 For example "Ancient Indictments," file 179, m. 105, printed in 1 Cyril Flower, *Public Works in Mediaeval Law* (Selden Society, vol. 32; London, 1915), 302.

26 Y.B. Mich. 1 Rich. 3, fo. 1, pl. 1 (1483).

27 1 Brooke, *Abridgment*, 118, pl. 8, citing 41 Ass. [pl.] 22.

was issuing it directly, attested by the Chief Justice and commanding that the record be sent *ubicunque fuerimus in Anglia* (wherever we may be in England)[28]—the identifying phrase of King's Bench writs.

So used, certiorari ordered the lower court to send up only the indictment or presentment itself. Normally it issued before the defendant's plea had been entered, indeed it might issue before the indictment was found.[29] The Elizabethan William Lambard places his discussion of certiorari between the chapter on informations and indictments, on the one hand, and the chapter on process on the other, and he considers it as an "impediment of proceeding upon enditements."[30] (After conviction, a writ of error might lie for the whole record.) In this respect the practice on certiorari was parallel to that on *recordari*, where only the bill or original writ was sent up even though the defendant's plea might have been entered.

When such a case came up for consideration in the King's Bench, the defendant could take only two types of legal objection at the outset. (1) He could object that the base court did not have jurisdiction to require him to answer the charge, or that the record did not fully make out their jurisdiction (as in the case cited above from the sheriff's turn). (2) He could object to the form or matter of the indictment. But he could also traverse the indictment and go to trial instead, and in the course of trial he could raise any other questions of fact or law that became relevant.

28 Controlment Rolls, *passim*.

29 Lambard, *Eirenarcha*, Book 4, c. 7, p. 516, citing Y.B. 1 Rich. 3, [fo.] 4.

30 *Ibid.*, p. 513.

The point to be noted is that at this stage of the case nothing about the lower court's proceedings had any relevance to the defendant's fate in King's Bench—no issues of law were presented—except its jurisdiction and the text of the indictment or presentment, the record sent up. But every issue of fact or law could be tried de novo if the defendant chose to traverse instead of demurring.

Seventeenth-Century Developments: Growth of the New Remedy

The story of the gradual emergence of certiorari "to quash" in the middle of the seventeenth century as a means of reviewing administrative orders is inherently complex. It begins with the activities of justices of peace, who as "Keepers of Peace" had been "a normal and stereotyped part of the machinery of government" since the reign of Edward II.[31] They had enforced economic legislation since the Black Death of 1357, beginning with the first Statutes of Laborers. They did so largely by the usual procedures of criminal justice: presentment, indictment or information, trial, verdict, and judgment.[32] In such cases review of their actions could be had by writ of error, or a case could be removed for trial in King's Bench by certiorari. In case of a monetary liability a man could also obtain review by allowing the sum to be levied against his property and then bringing an action in the central courts against the levying official. But this could be a very slow process.

As we have seen, a number of statutes between 1540

31 Bertha Putnam, *Proceedings before the Justices of Peace in the Fourteenth and Fifteenth Centuries* (London, 1938), p. xiii.

32 *Ibid., passim.*

and 1600 gave the justices of peace power to make certain types of orders, more or less administrative in kind. (1) The Act 5 & 6 Edward 6, c. 25, had already authorized them to license alehouses and "tippling-houses," to take bond from their keepers "as well against the using of unlawful Games, as also for the using and maintenance of good Order and Rule . . . within the same," and to punish those who sold ale and beer without license. (2) The Elizabethan Statute of Laborers, 5 Elizabeth c. 4, paragraph 35, *inter alia* authorized them to "take order" as between master and apprentice if either party complained, and on proper occasion to discharge an apprentice from his bond. (3) They were to order the reputed father of any bastard child to pay for its upkeep, by the statute 18 Elizabeth, c. 3. If the father refused to obey such an order by two justices, he was to be bound over to appear at the next general sessions of the peace and to abide by the order of the sessions. (4) The poor laws, 39 Elizabeth, c. 5, and 43 Elizabeth, c. 2, gave them very wide powers in connection with poor rates, poor relief, and the settlement of poor persons.

None of the existing legal remedies against actions of the justices were reliable or convenient to use in connection with these new administrative orders. It was not long, however, before more direct remedies were sought by the citizens affected. First, an attempt was made to use the developing writ of habeas corpus *ad subjiciendum* for this purpose. It was easy enough for any litigant to get himself committed "for his contempt" in his conduct before the justices, as the experience of William Ligarde before the Surrey and Kent sewers commissioners shows. The commissioners levied on part of a haystack of Ligarde's for money taxed against him by their order, and

Ligarde undoubtedly acted "contemptuously and in dispite of thauctority of this courte" in taking the hay back. But when Ligarde appeared in court, in the commissioner's view, he "arrogantly toke upon him to correct & allso to teache the commissioners ther duties first to telle them ther commission was determined & so more offence comitted. Then that the said collectors warrante should have ben Indented . . . so what the collector hath done he hath done it inorderly & without warrant with divers other such like arrogaunt tauntes in the face of the courte & in contempt of the quenes Maiesties commission."[33]

There are many examples in the Controlment Rolls from 1589 on of the use of habeas corpus as a means of reviewing the orders of justices of peace, and Bulstrode reports several such cases for the years 1627-1632.[34] But a remedy that can only be invoked by going to jail cannot be called convenient.

With so much introduction we may proceed to the remedy that was ultimately developed. Certiorari "to quash" emerged very gradually during the period 1635-1680 or thereabouts. The first step was the appearance of a new form of the writ, beginning "Volentes certis de causis quendam ordinem . . . certiorari" (Wishing for certain reasons to be informed about a certain order) by which these orders could be removed into Kings Bench. The second was a reassertion by King's Bench of its lapsed jurisdiction over commissioners of sewers, in a new form which led to novel results. At this point, in the mid-seventeenth century, it seems to have been at least

33 *London County Council, Surrey and Kent Commission*, p. 114.

34 *The King and Charles Hammonde*, 2 Bulstr. 341, *The King and Reve*, 2 Bulstr. 344, *The King and Smith*, 2 Bulstr. 342.

theoretically possible to go to trial at the bar of King's Bench after removing orders of justices or of sewers by certiorari. The true certiorari "to quash" did not appear until by a third step that possibility was eliminated, sometime before 1700. It is this gradual development which seems to explain the characteristic scope of review by King's Bench on certiorari, and it probably accounts for the striking lack of discussion of that problem during the seventeenth century.

The new form of certiorari for orders appears first in connection with the justices' power to take recognizances. Their ancient power to require security to keep the peace, to appear at the sessions, or to be of good behavior was founded on custom rather than statute. The authorities never discuss this procedure as a whole, but it appears to have been as follows:[35] A, who feared physical harm from B, could complain either to a justice of peace in the county or in Chancery, and have B summoned to put up security which would be forfeit if he broke the condition stated in the bond. If he complained in Chancery a writ of supplicavit would issue to the appropriate justices of peace, commanding them to summon B and take security from him. The justices then returned a certificate to the Chancery that they had done as they were commanded.

If B broke the condition of his recognizance, the grand jury at the next Sessions of the Peace might present or indict him, with or without complaint by A. Or—and this is the link with our story—A might make suggestion

35 The following paragraphs have been pieced together from the implications of Lambard, *Eirenarcha*, pp. 99, 103, 107, 108; *R. v. Leonard*, Palmer 322 (Mich., 20 Jac., 1622), and 2 Rol. Rep. 348 (Trin., 21 Jac., 1623); Y.B. M. 2 Hen. 7, pl. 2 (Tottell, 1555), and *Reg. Brevium*, fo. 151 *nota*. There is no clear account of the procedure, nor is the scattered evidence entirely conclusive.

in the Chancery of the breach. Certiorari would then issue out of the Chancery to call up the recognizance, B would be summoned, and he could traverse or demur in Chancery to the breach or to the making of the recognizance. The Chancery could then itself proceed to judgment on the bond; but it may be that for execution against the surety the case must be removed into King's Bench.[36] At least after 1585, however, the whole procedure on breach could in some cases take place from King's Bench. The controlment rolls after that year—and quite probably before—are full of orders of justices of the peace in such cases and of certioraris for recognizances.

To transform this activity on recognizances into a means of reviewing the "administrative" orders of justices of peace which we have described, three changes were necessary. First, the certiorari should issue on the motion of the party bound, *before* breach of the recognizance. Dalton's *Countrey Justice*,[37] published in 1618, shows that by that year this could be done, at least as to recognizances for good behavior and to keep the peace. Dalton's statement does not indicate the reason for doing this, but one may fairly infer that one result, at least, of removing a recognizance in this way was to test its legal validity. For the party bound could challenge it in proceedings after breach,[38] and if he himself moved to bring it up at an earlier stage, the motion must be presumed to benefit him, or at least not to hurt him.

Second, it was necessary that such a certiorari should issue for recognizances taken in connection with the

36 *Reg. Brevium*, fo. 151 *nota*.
37 Pages 146, 164.
38 *R. v. Leonard*, 2 Rol. Rep. 348 (Trin. 21 Jac., 1623).

various administrative orders that have been mentioned. It will be remembered that two of the four statutes authorizing these orders provide for recognizances as part of the enforcement routine. The first example which was found (earlier rolls were not searched) of certiorari in this connection dates from 1585[39] and calls up the recognizances of certain alehouse keepers. Seven years later the roll contains a certiorari for a paternity-order recognizance.[40] Here there is no indication of the purpose for which this was done, nor at which party's initiative, and so a broader jump becomes necessary to reach the conclusion I have suggested. It seems at least highly probable, however, that by about 1620 certiorari lay for recognizances based on these orders, at the option of the party bound, and for the purpose of testing their legal validity.

For the third step in this transformation there is direct evidence. In *Rex v. Justices of Marlborough*[41] five recognizances were called up by certioraris out of King's Bench, tested October 11 and October 13, 10 Charles (1634). These recognizances are on their face ordinary bonds to appear before the next general sessions and in the meantime to keep the peace. A week later certiorari issued again, not for a recognizance but for "a certain order" concerning bakers.[42] This is the new form of the writ, and hereafter it would issue without a previous recognizance. Note that both the certioraris in *Marlborough* must have issued on motion of the parties bound,

39 *R. v. Justices of Litchfield ex rel. Lovatt*, Controlment Roll no. 221, m. 93 (Pasch., 27 Eliz., 1585). There are probably also such certioraris in earlier rolls which were not examined.

40 Controlment Roll no. 230, m. 28 (Mich., 35 Eliz., 1592).

41 Controlment Roll no. 283, m. 125 (Mich., 11 Car., 1635).

42 The parties bound by the recognizances are described as bakers, the writs are addressed to the same justices of peace, and the entries follow one another consecutively.

for they follow too closely (under seventeenth-century conditions) on the making of the recognizances and the underlying order, which was dated October 6, to be proceedings on default or breach. Thus the underlying order of justices is brought up for review.

The text of the order[43] relates that a new market house has been built in the high street for the wool, butter, and cheese brought into Marlborough on market days, that the town bakers have been assigned another convenient place for their "standings" and nevertheless they have insisted on setting them up in the new market house. The justices therefore ordered that no baker should put his standing there without special license from the mayor and justices of peace, and if any should do so, he should find surety for his good behavior and appear at the next sessions.

The order in *Marlborough* was not based on any of the specific statutory powers of justices we have listed. Six weeks later, however, and again in the following year, certiorari issued for a bastardy order, and without any preceding recognizance.[44] Next, a writ tested 28 June, 13 Charles (1637), issued for an order discharging an apprentice from his master.[45] The first certiorari case under the poor laws—the area in which the great bulk of the seventeenth- and eighteenth-century cases fall—seems to have been in 1640.[46]

About this time the Court of King's Bench regained its

43 See Appendix C.

44 *R. v. London Justices,* Controlment Roll no. 283, m. 130 (Mich., 11 Car., 1635); writ tested 28 November, 10 Car. (1634); and *R. v. Shropshire Justices,* Controlment Roll no. 284, m. 230 (Hil., 11 Car., 1635/36).

45 *R. v. Justices of York,* Controlment Roll no. 286, m. 201 (Mich., 14 Car., 1638).

46 *R. v. St. Albans Justices,* Controlment Roll no. 289, m. 47 (Pasch., 16 Car., 1640).

removal jurisdiction over the commissioners of sewers. We have noted that in medieval times a presentment could be removed by certiorari from a sewers commission to the King's Bench, and there be tried de novo. Sometime before 1585 this jurisdiction lapsed, and no such certioraris isued from then until 1640.[47] Justice Mallet in 1642[48] suggested that the lapse of jurisdiction may have resulted from the statute 23 Henry 8, c. 5 (1531), because that statute gave the sewers commissions "a kind of legislative power" and permitted their proceedings to be in English instead of Latin.

The new form of certiorari for *quendam ordinem* which became available against sewers commissioners could be used to call up orders based on the commissioners' view of the work as well as presentments. The first sign that this was happening occurs in the controlment rolls for the years 1639-1641, in which several orders of sewers are enrolled without any indication how they came before King's Bench.[49] One of these entries contains only an order. A second entry consists of two presentments before sewers commissioners and three orders, followed by a note that a venire facias issued and the case was thereafter continued. A third entry contains only a presentment, again without indication how it concerns the King's Bench.

The first case in which it is certain that certiorari was used was *Rex v. Commissioners of Sewers of Yorkshire* in Michaelmas term 1641. Here the writ is a slight adaptation from the form used to remove presentments for trial: it calls for "omnes et singulas indictamentas . . .

47 Controlment Rolls, *passim*.

48 *Commins v. Massam*, March 196 at 197.

49 Controlment Rolls no. 287, m. 197 (Hil., 14 Car., 1638/39); no. 288, m. 118 (15 Car., 1639); and no. 289, m. 57 (Trin., 16 Car., 1640).

unacum omnibus ordinibus finibus sive amerciamentis unde Thomas Stephenson coram vobis facta presentatus fuit," to be sent up "coram nobis et non alibi terminari."[50]

Another certiorari issued in the following summer, to the commissioners of sewers for the River Thames from Ravensborne to Gravesend. It reads "Volentes certis de causis omnes et singulos ordines et decretas versus Henricum Puckering Baronet . . . coram nobis per vos mitteri." The entry in the roll is crossed out, with a notation "Sine die Pasch. 18 Car. Regis propter insufficienta presentamentum et decretum etc."[51] (This is probably the anonymous case reported by March[52] for Michaelmas term 17 Charles (1641), since it was under consideration from Trinity term 1641 to Easter 1642; but not enough details are reported to make the identification positive.)

Commins v. Massam

The entry for the remarkable case of *Commins v. Massam*[53] appears in the Easter term 1642. The writ takes the same form as that used against the Yorkshire commissioners a year earlier. This is the form used for removal, with the novel feature that proceedings after the presentment are specifically called for. In this case "Lessee

50 "All the indictments . . . along with all the orders, fines and amercements presented against Thomas Stephenson before you," "to be determined before us and not elsewhere." Controlment Roll no. 289, m. 151.

51 "Wishing for certain reasons that you should send before us all orders and decrees against Henry Puckering, Baronet," and "Dismissed Easter 18th year of King Charles because of insufficient presentment and decree." Controlment Roll no. 290, m. 59 (Trin., 17 Car., 1641).

52 March 123 (Mich., 17 Car., 1641).

53 *Comyns v. Maskam*, Controlment Roll no. 291, m. 39; *Commins v. Massam*, March 196 (Pasch., 18 Car., 1642).

for years of Lands . . . subject to be drowned by the Sea, covenanted to pay all assessments, charges and taxes, towards or concerning the reparation of the premisses." When a straight sea wall protecting this land was broken down by "a sudden and inevitable Tempest," the commissioners of sewers ordered a new wall to be built in the form of a horseshoe, and they taxed the costs of this new wall to the lands benefited. The whole of the share apportioned to the lands in question was taxed to the lessee and none to the owner, although the lease had nearly expired. The commissioners came to a decision on this case only after nearly ten years of argument, argument which must have attracted considerable attention from lawyers, for many sessions were held in the halls of the several inns of court. The last session before the commissioners was on February 7, 1639/40. Sometimes during the next two years the lessee's executor brought certiorari, and "the parties . . . by agreement bound themselves . . . in a recognisance to stand to the Judgment of this Court upon the proceedings as they are certified."[54]

Commins v. Massam is an outstanding illustration of the way in which the common law continued its steady development throughout the troubles of the Civil War and Interregnum. The case was enrolled in Easter term 1642, just after Charles' attempted arrest of the Five Members and only a few months before the armed conflict broke out. It was probably argued in the summer and fall of 1641, just before the Grand Remonstrance was debated in Parliament. As we shall see, two of the three judges were deeply committed in the struggle between King and Parliament; yet no sign of this appears in their opinions in this case.

Chief Justice Bramston was on the whole a moderate

54 Bramston, C.J., March 196 at 199.

parliamentarian, but when the case was argued he was temporarily in disgrace with Parliament. Thirteen years before he had defended Sir Robert Darnel and the other Five Knights from prosecution when they refused to make the King a forced loan, levied without Parliamentary authority. Two years later, in 1629, he had defended Sir John Eliot, Denzil Holles, and others when, for their part in drawing up the Petition of Right, they were prosecuted for seditious speeches, conspiracy, and contempt of the King. Nevertheless in 1635 Charles appointed Bramston Chief Justice of the King's Bench. His first act on his appointment was to advise Charles that he could legally levy ship money on all his kingdom, inland as well as sea port. In *John Hampden's Case* he voted against the King on a technical ground, but he made it clear that he had not changed his opinion on the main issue. For this opinion the Long Parliament impeached him in December 1640; and at the time *Commins v. Massam* was argued he was still under bond to attend Parliament from day to day until he should be tried. He was never tried, however; King Charles revoked his patent in October 1642. From then on Parliament first tried to force the King to reinstate him, and later tried to persuade him to take office under Cromwell; but Bramston resolutely avoided public affairs until his death in 1654.

Justices Heath and Mallet were royalists. Heath had been Attorney General from 1625 to 1630 and as such he had prosecuted the Five Knights and Eliot, Holles, and their fellows. In May 1642 he was to attend the King on his expedition to York, and he followed him to Oxford after the war had begun. Charles appointed him Chief Justice of the King's Bench in October 1642; later Parliament impeached him of high treason and he fled to France, where he died in 1649.

Mallet had supported the prerogative in Parliament in 1625, but did not attain prominence until he was appointed to the King's Bench in July 1641. In March 1642 he was hearing assizes in Maidstone, Kent. He "caused the grand jury of Kent, which, though he had selected its members himself, was with difficulty brought to complaisance," to petition against Parliament's doings, in favor of the Book of Common Prayer and against Parliamentary control of the militia. "[T]aking charge of the petition, he showed it to John Digby, first earl of Bristol, prior to laying it before Parliament. For this the lords committed him to the Tower, 28 March 1642, and it was not until 2 May that he was released." In the following summer he again angered Parliament, by refusing to allow its messenger to read certain votes aloud in court. Parliament sent a troop of horse to seize him from the bench, and he was again sent to the Tower, for over two years. He stayed in England after his release, however, survived the Interregnum, and was restored to the bench by Charles II in 1660, at the age of seventy-eight. He died five years later.[55]

But of all this there is no sign in *Commins v. Massam.* The three judges disagreed whether the case was properly removed by certiorari. Chief Justice Bramston, the moderate, thought the removal was proper. "But I confess, if I had thought of it, I would not have granted it [certiorari] so easily . . . I did not stick upon the *Certiorare,* because what was done was by consent, & *consensus tollit errorem,* if any be."[56] Justice Mallet, the royalist (who had himself served as a commissioner of

[55] *Dictionary of National Biography,* articles on Sir John Bramston, Sir Robert Heath, and Sir Thomas Malet (or Mallet).

[56] March 196 at 199.

sewers in Somerset), likened the commissioners to an inferior court of equity or to Parliament and thought that their proceedings could not properly be removed into King's Bench:

They have legislative power to make laws and ordinances which are returnable in Chancery, and therefore, I conceive they are not questionable here, neither by writ of error nor by any other route, but only in Parliament; and when their orders have the royal assent, they are like acts of Parliament. In London the Mayor's Court has a Chancery power; but if a case depending there should be removed to this Court by certiorari, I conceive that we have no power to intermeddle in it, for our power and commission is legal only. So in the case at bar: the proceedings are in an equitable, Chancery way, in such a Course that this Court has no Jurisdiction.[57]

Mallet argued that although there were precedents for the removal, they were all earlier than the statute of 23 Henry 8, c. 5. Before that statute the commissioners were known as justices and their proceedings, being in Latin, were reviewable by writ of error in the King's Bench; but since that statute their commission and proceedings are all in English, of which, under the statute 36 Edward 3, c. 15, a common-law court can take no notice. This argument appears to be derived from Robert Callis' *Reading on the Statute of Sewers*, given at Gray's Inn in 1622.[58]

Justice Heath, the former Attorney General, said that King's Bench could properly review the case:

I hold that the cause is well removed by the Certiorare, there is no Court whatsoever but is to be corrected by this

57 Harvard Law School (Turner) MS 113 at 170.

58 Harvard Law School L MS 1053, signed "Per me Robertum Callis Lectorem," f. 177; p. 234 of the first printed edition (1647).

Court. I agree that after the Statute no Writ of Error lieth upon their proceedings, but that proves not that a Certiorare lies not . . . Without question in trespass or Replevin their proceedings are examinable here, and I see no reason but upon the same ground in a *Certiorare*.[59]

After *Commins v. Massam* the new removal procedure quickly became popular; the Controlment Roll for 1649 alone contains fifteen examples of its use, although not more than four are in the printed reports. For the period 1642-1700 the reports contain over fifty cases and it is a fair inference that there were several hundred unreported cases.

Although much of the evolution of both certiorari and mandamus took place during the troubled years of the Civil War and the Interregnum, no one seems to have held it against them: their use and development continued unbroken after the Restoration. One mandamus case of 1651, cited in 1662, was dismissed with the comment "that being in the late troublesome times, the Court did not regard it."[60] But generally cases in Style and Siderfin, the two principal reporters of the Interregnum, are cited as freely and with the same respect as other cases—perhaps because the bar had generally supported both the Long Parliament and the Restoration.

Procedural Changes

In the first years after *Commins v. Massam*, the procedure in King's Bench on certiorari was twofold: The "appellant" might move to quash the order immediately, or the case could go to trial either after the motion to

59 March 196 at 197.

60 *Hurst's Case*, 1 Lev. 75, citing an unreported mandamus to restore an attorney in the borough court of Southwark.

quash had been denied or without any such motion. Style's *Practical Register* (1657), the first treatise to discuss these proceedings on certiorari at all, says:

> This Court hath authority to Quash Orders of Sessions, Presentments, Endictments &c made in inferior Courts, or before Justices of Peace or other Commissioners if there be cause, that is, if they be defective in matter or form . . . But this Quashing is but by favour of the Court, for the Court is not tyed Ex Officio to do it, but may leave the party to plead unto them, as in many cases they use to do.[61]

The motion to quash was of course entertained at motion sessions of the court and on motion days. It was procedurally earlier than the demurrer, although as Style suggests its scope was very similar. It raised every issue of law then presented, but as has been noted, the only such issues at that stage of the proceedings were the jurisdiction of the inferior court and errors "on the face" of the record before the court. It seems almost certain that this motion had been part of the medieval removal procedure.

By 1702, at least, a series of decisions and rules had eliminated, in most cases, the possibility of a trial at bar after certiorari for orders. After this elimination, a true certiorari to quash was left. Apparently it included even the typical pattern of review which was later made articulate and was theoretically current until very recently.

The elimination of the trial in King's Bench may be traced as follows, for sewers commissioners: In medieval times their procedure had consisted of presentment by a jury and order by the commissioners, without any further

61 William Style, *Regestum Practicale, Or, The Practical Register, Consisting of Rules, Orders and Observations . . . More Particularly Applicable to the Proceedings in the Upper Bench* (London, 1657), p. 272. This is the author of Style's *Reports*.

trial of the facts. The defendant could have certiorari to remove the presentment to King's Bench, but even so late as 1578 he could not traverse the presentment before the commissioners without express permission.[62] After 1640, as we have shown, he could also have certiorari to remove the order and other later proceedings as well as the presentment. Chief Justice Bramston's language in *Commins v. Massam* shows that he envisaged a trial in King's Bench after such a removal. He says that certiorari will lie:

> He held, as it was agreed before, That no Writ of Error lieth after this Statute, but yet he said that the party greived should be at no loss thereby; for he said, that where the party cannot have a Writ of Error, nor *Audita Querela,* there he shall be admitted to plead . . . where a man is not party to a judgment, there he cannot have a Writ of Error, but there he may falsifie, so I conceive that he may in this Case, because he cannot have a Writ of Error.[63]

Siderfin's note on *Lord Dunbar's Case,*[64] in 1662, shows that a "new trial" in King's Bench was still available at that date by one procedure or both. Four years later, in *Commissioners of Sewers v. Wilmore,*[65] the court refused certiorari for a presentment unless the applicant would make oath that the commissioners had refused to allow a traverse. The reason given by the applicant for granting certiorari, "in regard they could not try whether the Defendant ought to repair or not" is an objection to their usual procedure without trial. It cannot mean that the commissioners had no jurisdiction, for liability to repair sewers was precisely their province.

62 London County Council, *Surrey and Kent Commission,* pp. 283-285.
63 March 196 at 201.
64 1 Sid. 78 (Trin., 14 Car. 2, 1662).
65 2 Keb. 137 (Hil., 18 & 19 Car. 2, 1666/67).

Commissioners of Sewers v. Newburg[66] appears to be the final step which eliminated any trial at bar de novo for orders of sewers commissioners. This statement rests on an emendation of Keble's text for which there is not much evidence—except that it makes sense of a passage which, as it stands, is nonsense. Certiorari was brought on an order of sewers commissioners distraining the "appellant" for an acre tax, and "the defendant" justified in King's Bench. "And the Court conceived this not a fit way, being to put the Commissioners to enquire of the value of every Acre, but on Return of the Orders by *certiorari* this Court cannot determine it, but the Commissioners must, and in trespass or Trover it may be proper." This collection of contradictions becomes a sensible statement if it is read "being to put the Court to inquire of the value of every acre." Moreover, it becomes a more accurate statement of the law, for it was eminently the commissioners' business to make this inquiry, under *Rooke's Case*.[67] On this interpretation, *Newburg* declares that a trial of these facts is not available on certiorari for orders of sewers commissioners; and so only the motion to quash remains.

The orders of justices of peace which we have discussed were generally summary, without the formalities of presentment or trial. Most of them could be appealed to the sessions and the facts tried there. The earlier removal procedure had not applied to them, and it is not wholly clear that a full trial in King's Bench was ever available for all of these orders. Possibly here the scope of a motion to quash on certiorari was taken mainly by analogy to the practice on indictments or orders of sewers; yet in

66 3 Keb. 827 (Mich., 29 Car. 2, 1677).
67 5 Co. 99b (C.B., Hil., 40 Eliz., 1597/98). Above, note 52, Chapter I.

that case one would expect more discussion of the problem in the literature. A case in 1652 shows that in some instances a trial at bar could then be had after certiorari for sessions orders. In this case a man chosen constable by the quarter sessions removed their order to the upper bench and moved to quash it; "but the Court would not do it although ther were material exceptions taken against it, but ordered him to plead, because they perceived the party was stubborn, and they would not give encouragement to such persons."[68] But *The King v. Sherwin*,[69] in 1669, indicates that by that date a trial of fact was usually not available: here the court refused to issue a certiorari because a practice of the sessions in relation to apprentices "being a setled course, is not to be overthrown by motion but by trial." At least by 1702 and probably much earlier, a general rule was made that no certiorari would lie for orders of justices until the time for an appeal to the sessions had expired.[70] Presumably this was for the same reason that Chief Justice Holt gave in restating the rule, some years later, "This Court cannot meddle in matters of fact."[71]

Certiorari as a Discretionary Writ

The discretionary element in certiorari follows naturally from its origin as a preliminary motion in removal proceedings. The motion to quash was discretionary in the 1650's and presumably before; but the effect of denying the motion was only procedural at that time, since it

68 *Anonymous*, Style 358 (Mich. 1652).

69 2 Keb. 480 (Pasch., 21 Car. 2, 1669).

70 *Regula Generalis*, 1 Salk. 147 (1702). A trial of fact was of course available at sessions.

71 *The King v. Inhabitants of Ailesbury*, Fort. 309 (undated).

was followed by pleading and trial. The first reported case showing the element of discretion, the case of the stubborn constable, above, illustrates this point. In *Lord Dunbar's Case* in Trinity term 1662,[72] certiorari issued for an order of sewers, but the court refused to act on it unless the complainant would do the repairs ordered and take his chances on being reimbursed later. A few years later the court apparently refused to issue a certiorari at all on an order of sewers unless the "plaintiff" would make affidavit that the sea wall in question was not dangerous.[73] The court also refused to issue certiorari on exceptions to such orders "that are onely mispleading."[74] In 1724 one Arthur was removed as clerk to the commissioners of sewers for Yorkshire, and the court held that in such a case a certiorari was "of common right, and not discretionary, as in the case of other orders, where great inconveniencies may follow by inundations in the mean time."[75]

Certiorari to justices of peace was withheld in 1669 for the sake of a more appropriate procedure, because the action complained of "being a settled course is not to be overthrown by motion but trial."[76] In *Dom. Rex v. Inhabitants of Uttoxeter* the writ was denied to bring up the poor rate itself, probably because no money could be raised or spent under the rate once it was sent up to Westminster, and so the poor would suffer.[77]

72 1 Sid. 78 (Trin., 14 Car. 2, 1662).

73 *The King and Day v. Commissioners of Sewers*, 2 Keb. 129 (Mich., 18 Car. 2, 1666).

74 *The King and Heart v. Commissioners of Sewers*, 2 Keb. 339 (Pasch., 20 Car. 2, 1668).

75 *Case of the Commissioners of Sewers for Yorkshire*, 1 Stra. 609 (1724).

76 *The King v. Sherwin*, 2 Keb. 480 (Pasch., 21 Car. 2, 1669).

77 2 Stra. 932 (1731), also reported 2 Barnard. K.B. 83, W. Kel. 186.

To What Courts or Agencies Does Certiorari Lie?

Certiorari was not readily available at the beginning of Queen Anne's reign to review the acts of inferior courts, quasi-courts, or quasi-administrative agencies. Chief Justice Holt's often quoted language in *Groenvelt v. Burwell* is misleading in its sweep. We have seen that the writ developed in relation to justices of peace and commissioners of sewers; but both of these are courts of record to which the certiorari for removal would lie in medieval times.

In 1666 the court refused to review the proceedings of the commissioners of the fens, a body which had been set up by the statute 15 Charles 2, c. 17 (1663), to decide claims to land in the newly drained Great Level of East Anglia. Some claims were made out through the Earl of Bedford, to whom large amounts of land were due in return for his successfully draining the fens. Other claimants were "squatters" who had had peaceful possession of the land, in some cases for many years. The Court said, refusing to take jurisdiction: "This is a new and absolute Judicature in the Commissioners by this new Law with which this Court has nothing to do if they proceed according to the Statute for then this obliges perpetually. But if they do not proceed according to the Statute, then everything is void, and *coram non judice*, and the parties are free to examine this in an action brought at the Common Law."[78]

Rex v. Corpus Winchelsea[79] was a certiorari to the

78 *Ball v. Pattridge*, 1 Sid. 296 (Trin., 18 Car. 2, 1666). In the same case reported in 2 Keb. at 82, the Court said "because this Court can do nothing, as in the Commissioners of Sewers, which are at common law, they can; but this case is like the Commission of Bankrupts, in which case, if they decree *contra* to law, the party hath his remedy by action."

79 3 Keb. 154, Freeman 99, 2 Lev. 86 (Pasch., 25 Car. 2, 1673).

mayor and jurats of Winchelsea for an order "whereby they had taxed the Foreign [landholders]; and they return, that they had made Taxes for the Foreign for the Preservation of the Corporation, and to raise Ammunition to provide against Invasion of Foreigners." The corporation then returned its privilege as a member of the Cinque Ports "ubi breve domini Regis non currit" (where the King's writ does not run). This return was quashed, and the corporation was then allowed to make a second return of the merits of the case. The court had decided before this that habeas corpus would lie to the Cinque Ports, despite their privileged position. So also would certiorari to remove pleas touching the King's revenue or indictments for felony, but not certiorari to remove the ordinary civil plea "between party and party."[80] Chief Justice Hale said that this case, being between the corporation and its landowners, involved "matters of a middle nature, as where the King and his subjects are both concerned," and so certiorari would lie. The mayor and jurats were a court of record, at least by a grant of Charles I and probably much earlier.

Five years later a certiorari issued to the Merchant-Taylors Company of London, one of the great livery companies with many quasi-public functions, and was returned by them without protest.[81] In this case the writ was probably auxiliary to a habeas corpus, however, and not a part of the present story.

The next stage in the expansion of certiorari to quash was the work of Chief Justice Holt. Sir John Holt, Chief Justice of England under William III and Queen Anne,

80 Cf. *Hopestill Tyndal's Case*, Cro. Car. 264 (Trin., 8 Car., 1632) and *Bourne's Case*, Cro. Jac. 543 (Mich., 17 Jac., 1619).

81 *The King v. the Merchant-Taylors of London*, 2 Lev. 200 (Trin., 29 Car. 2, 1677).

is perhaps best remembered for his rulings in 1701-1710 that slavery could not exist in England—anticipating Lord Mansfield's decision by seventy years.[82] Every department of the law, from the conduct of criminal trials to the definition of Parliament's privileges, felt Holt's influence; in fact if, as Holdsworth says, "the Revolution [of 1688] was essentially the victory of the lawyers and Parliament,"[83] then Holt's career embodied and developed that settlement, with its trust in Parliament and the common law as supreme. His personal character is illustrated by the story that when he was offered the Lord Chancellorship in 1700, he declined it, saying that "he had never had but one Chancery cause in his life, which he lost, and consequently he could not think himself fitly qualified for such a trust."[84]

Holt's dicta in two great cases at the turn of the century have been taken as the leading cases or jumping-off points for the modern law of certiorari. In the *Case of Cardiff Bridge*[85] one question was whether certiorari would lie to justices of peace in Wales. Holt held that it would, saying "wherever any new jurisdiction is erected, be it by private or public act of parliament, they are subject to the inspections of this Court by writ of error, or by *certiorari* and *mandamus*." In Lord Raymond's account, Holt distinguished this case from that of commissioners in bankruptcy who "had only an authority, and not a jurisdiction." It is to be noted, however, that even Welsh justices of peace are a court of record.

The second and more interesting case, decided in the

[82] Cf. 6 Holdsworth, *H.E.L.*, 265 n. 2-4.
[83] 6 Holdsworth, *H.E.L.*, 274.
[84] *Ibid.*, 517.
[85] 1 Salk. 146, 1 Ld. Raym. 580 (Trin., 12 Will. 3, 1700).

same term, was *Groenvelt v. Burwell.*[86] This was an action for false imprisonment against the censors of the College of Physicians of London. The semi-public body, in modern terms part trade union and part licensing board, had fined and imprisoned Dr. Groenvelt for malpractice of medicine in London, specifically for administering "pernicious pills and noxious drugs." The plaintiff asked leave to traverse their findings of malpractice, saying that otherwise he would have no remedy against their unjust judgment—following Coke's argument a century earlier in *Dr. Bonham's Case,*[87] an almost exact parallel to his own. This would have been his proper course in challenging an order of commissioners of bankruptcy, for example. Chief Justice Holt said, nevertheless, that the censors' judgment was not traversable,

> for persons who are Judges by law, shall not be liable to have their judgments examined in actions brought against them. Now it is plain that the censors have judicial power . . . where a man has power to inflict imprisonment upon another for punishment of his offense, there he hath judicial authority . . . where there is a jurisdiction erected de novo with power to fine and imprison, it is a Court of Record, for Courts of Record only can fine.

He thought Dr. Groenvelt could have had a certiorari:

> He compared it to convictions before justices of peace out of sessions, upon which, though error does not lie, yet a *certiorari* lies; for it is a consequence of all jurisdictions to have their proceedings returned here by *certiorari* to be examined here. . . . Where any Court is erected by statute, a *certiorari* lies to it.

86 1 Ld. Raym. 454, 1 Comyns 76, 1 Salk. 144, 200, 12 Mod. 145 (1679-1700).

87 8 Co. 114 (Hil., 7 Jac., 1609/10).

But he weakened the effect of these remarks by adding:

> If no *certiorari* lay, it does not follow, that because their proceedings are not examinable, that therefore they are not a Court of Record, for their jurisdiction is not diminished, because there is no appeal from it, but it is the stronger, because so great a trust is reposed in them.[88]

In spite of this last caveat, *Groenvelt v. Burwell* has been generally taken to mean that certiorari would lie to any "jurisdiction" with power to imprison or fine. Holt's definition of a court of record, following Coke in *Dr. Bonham*, appears to be somewhat more extensive than, for instance, the sixteenth-century conception.

Up to the year 1701, therefore, there had been no case in which certiorari to quash issued to a body which was not a court of record in some aspect of its work. It is to be remembered that the orders here discussed are very different from the judicial business "between party and party" which is characteristic of courts of record; nevertheless no case has been found up to at least 1760 in which certiorari actually issued to a body which was clearly not a court of record. It was possible so late as 1894 for the distinguished judge Lord Wright to say: "The writ of *certiorari* is applicable to judicial proceedings of courts, but the county council is not a court, and its proceedings are not judicial";[89] and in England it remained for the twentieth century to develop the doctrine that an administrative body may "act judicially" and its "judicial acts" are reviewable.

88 1 Ld. Raym. at 467, 469.

89 *Reg. v. London County Council: Re. The Empire Theatre*, 71 L. T. R. 638 at 640 (1894).

IV

JURISDICTION AND LEGALITY: THE WRITS OF PROHIBITION AND MANDAMUS

By about 1675 the new writ of mandamus had been used for many other purposes besides restitution to office. By that time also the new certiorari to quash was fairly clearly marked off from the traditional certiorari to remove for trial. For the development of both new writs after 1660 the elusive notion of jurisdiction was crucial. Mandamus made use of this concept as it had developed in the law of prohibition; while on certiorari the jurisdiction of the lower court had been one of the few issues of law presented by the medieval removal procedure, so that it was now clearly available to the "appellant." Some discussion of the general notion of jurisdiction, and an attempt to formulate its meaning in this context will therefore be useful at this point.

In modern legal theory the power of a court to deal with a case at all is made to depend in the main on three elements: its jurisdiction of the territory in which the cause of action arose (in one way or another); its power over the defendant's person; and its jurisdiction of the subject matter of the controversy. If all these conditions are satisfied, the court has jurisdiction, and even a decision that is clearly wrong cannot be overturned except by appeal to a higher court (if any) within the time allowed for such an appeal. If the court lacks jurisdiction in any of these ways, however, another court may treat its decision as wholly void and decide the controversy anew.

But the logic of a court's position as a decider of cases demands that the court should be able to know at the outset of a case whether it has jurisdiction. All the participants waste their time when a court hears a case and renders a decision which is later held to be void, or when it appears in the middle of a trial that the court has no jurisdiction. It follows that jurisdiction ought not to be made to depend on the remedy a court may order, on its findings of fact at intermediate stages of the case, or the procedural steps it may take. Provided that the plaintiff makes a sufficient statement to entitle the court to jurisdiction at the outset, questions which arise at later stages ought generally to be treated as matter of law, so that if the court follows a wrong rule of decision, its action can be reversed on appeal but cannot be avoided by collateral attack.

Classical legal doctrine departs from these considerations in a number of instances. Perhaps the most striking example is found in the phrase "equity jurisdiction." A court of equity was said to have jurisdiction to order particular remedies such as specific performance of contracts, or to give relief against fraud or breach of confidence. Another exception to these considerations is the classical doctrine—if it can be called anything so systematic—of jurisdiction on review by certiorari.[1]

1 Cf. Zechariah Chafee, Jr., *Some Problems in Equity*, chapters 8-9, and J. A. G. Griffith and H. Street, *Principles of Administrative Law*

These departures from the practical considerations which we find compelling are remnants of more primitive legal thinking. Seventeenth-century judges seem to have conceived of the division of business between the various courts of nation-wide power as depending on the body of law which was to be put into execution. For the hierarchy of spiritual courts this meant the canon law of the Church of England; for the "common-law" courts, the case law evidenced "in our books" and the statutes enacted by Parliament. For the Court of Chancery it meant certain kinds of legal relief in cases where the common law afforded no adequate remedy. Under such a scheme of classification jurisdiction will often coincide with subject matter; thus cases concerning rights in freehold land are for the common-law courts, while wills and testaments of personal property are for the spiritual courts. But the determining factor is the presence or absence of a rule of law that has been traditionally enforced in one court or the other. Thus it is perfectly proper to say that precisely because the common-law courts do not admit the defense of fraud in debt on a sealed instrument, therefore equity has jurisdiction to enjoin the fraudulent plaintiff in such a case from enforcing his common-law judgment.

This conception of jurisdiction as power to enforce a body of law is not often expressed, though it seems to underlie much that we find anomalous in seventeenth-century judicial reasoning. Justice Mallett's statement in *Commins v. Massam* will be remembered: "In London the Mayor's Court has a Chancery power; but if a case depending there should be removed to this Court by

(London, 1952), pp. 205-219. Cf. also the Norris–La Guardia Act, 29 U.S.C.A. 101 et seq.: "No court of the United States . . . shall have jurisdiction to issue any restraining order or . . . injunction . . . except in a strict conformity with the provisions of this chapter."

certiorari, I conceive that we have no power to intermeddle in it, for our power and commission is legal only. So in the case at bar, the proceedings are in an equitable, Chancery way, in such a Course that this Court has no Jurisdiction." In an early mandamus case the writ was refused because "as there is no law which says to whom these administrations during minority shall be granted, there is no law to be put into execution."[2]

Prohibition

The Court of King's Bench, where pleas were in theory heard "before the King himself," *coram rege ipso,* had the function of keeping other courts "in their jurisdiction." The ancient writ of prohibition was the means of doing this: it issued on suggestion in the King's Bench that the complainant was being sued in a court which had no jurisdiction to deal with the matter in controversy. That court could then be heard, and if it succeeded in making out its jurisdiction, a writ of consultation would issue from King's Bench to allow it to proceed in the case.

Prohibition was most commonly used against the spiritual courts. As we have suggested, the line of demarcation between spiritual and temporal courts was usually based on subject matter; most of the cases, therefore, say merely that the matter in controversy is temporal and therefore the church courts should be prohibited

[2] *Smith's Case,* 2 Stra. 892 (1731). Cf. also *The King v. Bishop of Litchfield,* 7 Mod. 217 (1734). The jurisdiction of local courts was defined by grant or prescription, and might be limited according to the territory in which the cause of action arose, as well as to cases under the jurisdictional amount of forty shillings; and by their overriding duty not to encroach on cases properly heard in the central courts. But other lines might be drawn: a borough court might be the only court in which the freemen of the borough could be sued, by grant or prescription; and the lord of a manor might have the right to decide all cases between his tenants.

from deciding it, or it is spiritual matter and prohibition ought not to issue.[3] But in at least three general situations King's Bench used its writ of prohibition to insure a right result, according to common law rules, in the spiritual court.

First, where a somewhat artificial dividing line between lay and spiritual matters had been drawn down the middle of a single subject matter or practical situation, the common-law courts might use the writ of prohibition to force the spiritual courts to make due allowance for common-law rules. Thus the probate of wills, appointment of administrators, and payment of legacies were spiritual matters, but payment of debts due to and from a decedent's estate was temporal. Before the Statute of Distributions, once a will was admitted to probate or an administrator named for an intestate, the executor or administrator could be sued at any time up to his death for debts of the testator. To protect him it was felt necessary that a grant of probate to an executor should be irrevocable or nearly so;[4] that in suits for legacies in the spiritual courts the executor should be able to plead and prove *Plene administravit* (fully administered) by the same rules as in actions of debt in the temporal courts;[5] and that he should not be compellable to distribute the decedent's goods to his family.[6] Prohibition would issue to enforce any of these rules.

Second, if, in a suit for a spiritual cause, a temporal question came collaterally into issue, the rule was some-

[3] Rolle, *Abridgment*, "Prohibition," *passim*.

[4] *Hill v. Mills et al.*, 1 Show. K.B. 293 (Trin., 3 W. & M., 1691). Cf. *Offley v. Best*, 1 Sid. 370 (Trin., 20 Car. 2, 1668).

[5] *Warner v. Barret*, Hetley 87 (Pasch., 4 Car., 1628, C.B.)

[6] *Hill v. Bird*, Style 102 (Pasch., 24 Car., 1648); *Hughes v. Hughes*, 1 Lev. 233 (Hil., 19 & 20 Car. 2, 1667/68).

what uncertain. Coke's opinion in *Parker v. Kemp*[7] appears to have been "the better view": such questions could be tried in the spiritual court, but that court must follow common-law rules of law and evidence. "If they will judge in Common Law matters otherwise then we do, there in such cases we will prohibit them." Justice Dodderidge took this view in the case of a libel for a *modus decimandi* (a money payment in composition of tithes): "if the parson do libel in the Spiritual Court for a *modus decimandi* (as he may do) and another *modus* is there suggested, and this refused, they may there try and determine this matter . . . and no cause to grant a Prohibition for this refusal: But if they do there refuse the suggestion for the *modus* upon this ground, because their law and our law do differ in the point of proof; as for default of two Witnesses, one being allowable in our Law, but not with them: In this case a prohibition is to be granted." The rest of the court seems to have thought, however, that prohibition should go simply because the terms of the *modus*, being a temporal agreement, had come in issue.[8] Yet it was clear that a person could sue on a *modus* in the spiritual court.

Third, by far the most important case from our point of view, if an Act of Parliament prescribed rules of decision or procedure for the ecclesiastical courts, prohibition would issue to enforce the statute. There were a surprising number of such statutes even in medieval times, and more during the Reformation.

For instance, tithes—the parson's right to one tenth of his parishioners' crops and other earnings—are pre-emi-

7 2 Bulstr. 227, Pasch., 12 Jac. (1614). Cf. also *Juxon v. Lord Byron*, 2 Lev. 64, Trin., 24 Car. 2 (1672).

8 *Harding v. Goseling*, 3 Bulstr. 241 (Mich., 14 Jac., 1616).

nently a spiritual matter. But the temporal courts at least sometimes determined what things were titheable. Thus it was argued that prohibition would issue against suits in the spiritual court for tithes of dead tree roots, of stone quarries, brick, or clay "because it is *ad exhaeredationem*, and utter destruction" of the freehold.[9] Again, the statute 45 Edward 3, c. 3 (1371), provided that a prohibition should go against claims for tithes of great woods (certain kinds of trees cut for timber). Viner's *Abridgment*, "Dismes (Q),"[10] cites a large number of prohibition cases on this statute.

A series of statutes dating from the Reformation[11] provided in considerable detail for payment of tithes and the like "according to the Ecclesiastical lawes and ordinances of his [the King's] Church of England, and after the laudable usages and customes of their parish." Under the authority of this provision the temporal courts took it on themselves to decide, on suggestion, whether a parish had a custom that particular products should not be titheable, and to issue prohibition if such a custom was found. *Norton v. Fermer*[12] may be given as an example: "Prohibition was granted to stay a suit for tithe of wood, upon surmise that the wood was spent in his house for firing; and shews, that the custom in the same parish is, that the owners of any house and land in the said parish . . . ought not to pay tithes of wood spent for fuel in their houses. Issue being upon this custom, it was found for the defendant."

[9] *Skinner's Case*, March 58 and 64 (Mich., 15 Car., 1639). Charles Viner, in 8 *General Abridgement of Law and Equity* (London, 1791), 569, note, says it does not appear that prohibition was ever granted in this case.

[10] Vol. 8, p. 572.

[11] Stat. 27 Hen. 8, c. 20; 32 Hen. 8, c. 7; 2 & 3 Edw. 6, c. 13.

[12] Cro. Car. 113 (Trin., 4 Car., 1628).

Another Reformation statute, 25 Henry 8, c. 19, paragraph 2, provided "No canons [laws of the Church] . . . shall bee made or put into execution within this Realme, by authority of the Convocation of the Clergie, which shall be contrariant or repugnant to the king's prerogative Royall, or the customes, laws or Statutes of this realm." From it followed *inter alia* the case of the *Parishioners of Rolvedon, Kent,*[13] adjudged in 1607. "If the parishioners of a parish have used time whereof memory, etc. to elect one churchwarden, and the vicar another, and a canon is made that the vicar shall elect both, and he does accordingly, and the parishioners elect one according to the custom, and the ordinary disallows him, and establishes the two elected by the vicar, a prohibition shall be granted."

The cases on the statute 32 Henry 8, c. 38, show a change which seems to have taken place in the late seventeenth century. The act provides that every marriage contracted between lawful persons, solemnized in the face of the Church, and consummate with bodily knowledge, "shalbe . . . taken to be lawful, good, just and indissoluble . . . and that no reservation, or prohibition, God's law except, shall trouble or impeach any marriage without the leviticall degrees. And that no person . . . shall . . . bee admitted to any of the spirituall Courts . . . to any processe, plea or allegation contrary to this foresaid Act." In 1670 it seems to have been clear that prohibition lay upon this act, for it issued in *Harrison v. Burwell,*[14] and Justice Vaughan, announcing the decision, said that he spoke

13 17 Viner, *Abridgement,* 567, pl. 50 (Pasch., 5 Jac., 1607). Cf. also *Parish of Ethelburrow,* March 22 (Pasch., 15 Car., 1639), and other cases cited in Viner.

14 2 Ventr. 9 (Trin., 22 Car. 2, 1670). Cf. also 15 Viner, *Abridgement,* 255, "Marriage (E)."

for "all the Judges of England." But only twelve years later prohibition in a similar (though closer) case was "denied by the whole Court, because it is a cause of ecclesiastical cognizance, and divines better know how to expound the law of marriages than the common lawyers; and though sometimes prohibitions have been granted in causes matrimonial, yet if it were now *Res integra*, they would not be granted."[15]

It may be that the statute 21 Henry 8, c. 5 (1529), was the most productive of this sort of litigation; certainly it was the basis for one of the earliest uses of mandamus. It provided, as to wills and administrations, "That the said Ordynary, or other person or persons having auctority to take probate of testaments as is above said, shall graunt the Administracion of the Goods of the testatour or person disseased to the Wydow . . . the next of his kyn or both, as by the discrecion of the same Ordynary shalbe thought good" in the case of intestacy, and shall grant probate of any will lawfully proved before him. The courts held that prohibition would issue on a showing that the administrator named by the ordinary was not the proper person under the statute, and King's Bench had the final word on the interpretation of the statute. For instance, prohibition might go when administration was committed to the widow, on a showing in King's Bench that the deceased had an earlier wife living.[16] When administration was committed to a half-brother, prohibition issued on the suit of a brother of the whole blood, "to try the law on this by our law."[17] In *Fotherby's Case*[18]

15 *Watkinson v. Mergatron*, T. Raym. 464 (Pasch., 34 Car. 2, 1682).

16 *Betsworth and Betsworth*, Style 10 (Pasch., 23 Car., 1647).

17 *Wingate v. Finch*, 2 Rolle, Abridgment, 303, pl. 27 (Mich., 21 Jac., 1623).

18 Cro. Car. 62, Hil. 2 Car. But see *Levanne's Case*, Cro. Car. 201, Mich., 6 Car. (1630) for a different reason for the prohibition.

(1626/27) it was said that because of this statute, the ordinary had no authority to compel an administrator to make distribution of the estate, once administration was committed—a consequence Henry VIII's Parliament surely never intended.[19]

In these cases in which prohibition is used to control the results reached by spiritual courts in spiritual matters, there is almost no discussion of general legal theory—none at all until *Offley v. Best* (1668).[20] The cases reason primarily from precedent, as for example, "it is usual in prohibitions to allege customs."[21] Indeed, it is a significant fact that no treatise of the sixteenth, seventeenth, or even eighteenth centuries attempted to analyze the conception of jurisdiction in general. Such books as Crompton's *Jurisdiction of Courts*, Fitzherbert's *Diversity of Courts*, and Coke's *Fourth Institute* describe or catalogue the jurisdiction of particular courts. There is no general theory of jurisdiction in Coke's *Second Institute*,

19 It is an interesting fact that the only pre-Restoration prohibition I have seen which was addressed to a non-judicial agency concerned the enforcement of a statute:

"The Prior of E. brought attachment upon a prohibition against the Collectors of Tenths and Fifteenths [taxes] and counted that he delivered to them a Prohibition . . . that they should not distrain for certain rents issuing out of certain tenements held of him in London; and notwithstanding this they had taken certain sums of rents of certain of the tenants of the prior . . . They justified for tithes arising out of the lands of the religious, purchased after 21 E. I because the ward in London, in which the tenements lay, was not sufficient of goods, they took the rent of the tenants, because the day of payment was come, and because the tenants had paid the fifteenth for their goods, therefore per Cur. the prior shall not pay tenth for the same tenements, and therefore the defendants were condemned, and the damages taxed to 10 £ and the collectors *capiantur*"—Y.B. 7 Hen. 4 fo. 33b (1405) as slightly condensed in 18 Viner, *Abridgement*, at 58.

An analogy to this case may be found in *Breedon v. Gill*, 5 Mod. 272 (Mich., 8 W. 3, 1696).

20 1 Sid. 370 (Trin., 20 Car. 2, 1668).

21 *Norton v. Fermer*, Cro. Car. 113 (1628).

in Fitzherbert's *Novel Natura Brevium*, nor in Hale or even Blackstone. But if, as I have suggested, judges at this time sometimes thought of their jurisdiction as their power and duty to enforce a body of law, most of the cases can be defended. To us they seem anomalous since they cannot be subsumed under our more sharply defined and utilitarian notions of jurisdiction. But in the seventeenth century it must have been nearly impossible to distinguish jurisdictional matters from questions of law in general. Justice Heath made a gallant attempt to distinguish the sewers commissioners' "Jurisdiction" from their "Justice" in *Commins v. Massam,* but he found the difference extremely elusive.

Mandamus

It was the near identity of jurisdictional and legal questions under the earlier scheme that allowed the development of mandamus, by analogy with prohibition, into a means of obtaining any legal right for which no other remedy was provided. The comparison to the older writ was made as early as 1619, by Coke's successor, Chief Justice Montague (who thus asserted as strongly as Coke himself the supremacy of the common law over every one *except* the king). He said in the *Case of the Parish of S. Balaunce in Kent:*[22]

> When they in the Spiritual Court have acted contrary to our law, prohibition lies to them *de non procedendo*; the same law, as he understands it, when they have omitted to do something which by law they ought to do, there the King's Court will command them to do what pertains to the law.

In Rolle's report of the same case, Montague draws other analogies as well:

22 Palmer 50, Mich., 17 Jac.

This Court has jurisdiction over the Ecclesiastical Judge for his non-feasance or for his misfeasance, for a writ will be directed to the Bishop on his refusal to absolve an excommunicated person, see the writ *de cautione admittenda* . . . thus a writ shall be directed to the Lord of a Manor commanding him to hold Court so that Justice may be done to his tenants, in 11 Co. *Bagge's Case,* a writ to restore an Alderman directed to the Corporation . . . and although the Spiritual Court has cognizance, and power to swear him, yet their contempt in refusing gives Jurisdiction to the Court of King's Bench.[23]

It will be noted that the freehold theory of mandamus could be treated as an aspect of such an analogy to prohibition: freehold is a lay matter and prohibition will lie when the spiritual courts do anything to burden or affect the freehold. At this time it would lie when the right to a freehold office came in question, even though both parties claimed under the letters patent of a high clergyman.[24] For the same reasons, restitution or mandamus would lie.

Next should be noted a series of otherwise completely baffling cases in which mandamus is used in new fact situations without any articulate *ratio decidendi.* Each of these cases concerns the enforcement of a common-law or statutory right. They have no other common denominator, but some of them have close or exact precedents in the law of prohibition. In *S. Balaunce,* the parishioners had elected a church warden according to their custom, but the appropriate church official had refused to admit him. There is ringing language in the case, "for this is the office of the Supreme Justice, to command that justice

23 2 Rol. Rep. 106, sub nom. *Bishopp's Case.*

24 *Kiste v. Bridgman,* 2 Rolle, *Abridgment,* 285, pl. 36 (Mich., 15 Jac., 1617).

be done in the inferior courts, when there is negligence, and to restrain them when they pass their bounds and limits." But *S. Balaunce* is not fully intelligible until it is compared with the *Parishioners of Rolvedon*[25] and other cases on the statute 25 Henry 8, c. 19, paragraph 2. It is precisely analogous to those cases; the new writ of restitution, like prohibition, is being used to enforce the statute.

Luskins v. Carver[26] (where the new writ was first called mandamus) was the first case in which mandamus issued to a spiritual court to command it to appoint the executor named in a will (without making conditions on the appointment). The court "were of clear opinion that they might do it" without giving any reasons. But this ruling followed naturally from the statute 21 Henry 8, c. 5, and the cases thereon, since by the statute probate must be granted if a will was lawfully proved, and only the executor named in a will could lawfully prove it.

That King's Bench could command the ordinary to grant administration of an intestate's goods to his next of kin was first suggested by Chief Justice Montague in *S. Balaunce.* Mandamus issued for this purpose in 1658, in an anonymous case which both paraphrases Montague's language and cites the statute 21 (miscited 27) Henry 8.[27]

Again in 1668/69 a new use was made of mandamus without giving a reason: "It was moved for a prohibition with *mandamus* to the Spiritual Court of York to absolve one whom they had taken by *excommunicato capiendo* because he did not answer when he could not procure a copy of the articles against him.—*Et ea de causa et non*

25 17 Viner, *Abridgement*, 567, pl. 50 (1607).
26 Style 7 (Mich., 22 Car., 1646).
27 *Anonymous*, 2 Sid. 114, Mich. 1658, U.B.

alia—it was granted."[28] King's Bench intervened with two complementary remedies to enforce the statute 2 Henry 5, c. 3 (1414), "that at what time the libell [in the spiritual courts] is grantable by the law, that it may be granted and delivered to the party without any difficultie."

At the same time, in strictly spiritual matters not regulated by temporal law or affected by it, neither prohibition nor mandamus would issue. No mandamus lies to restore a proctor (attorney) in the spiritual courts, for "they are Judges of their own officers."[29] No mandamus lies to compel the spiritual court to grant probate of a contested will, for the statute 21 Henry 8 does not decide what wills are valid.[30] Nor does it lie as to administrations during the minority of an executor named in a will, "as there is no law which says to whom these administrations during minority shall be granted, there is no law to be put into execution."[31] It does not lie to a bishop in the exercise of his power as visitor of a cathedral chapter,[32] nor to compel him to license any person to hold lectures in a parish church, where no salary is annexed to the lectureship and therefore no temporal right can be involved.[33]

The scores of cases dealing with restoration to office may be seen as an extension or another aspect of this analogy. Since municipal offices are temporal, King's

28 *Taylor v. Spiritual Court of York*, 1 Sid. 403, 2 Keb. 352 (Hil., 20 & 21 Car. 2, 1668/69).

29 *Dom. Rex v. Oxenden*, 1 Show. K.B. 217, 219 (Trin., 3 W. & M., 1691), also reported sub nom. *Mr. Leigh's Case*, 3 Mod. 332.

30 *Dom. Rex v. Bettesworth*, 2 Stra. 857 (1730).

31 *Smith's Case*, 2 Stra. 892 (1731).

32 *R. v. Bishop of Chester*, 1 Wils. K.B. 206 (1747).

33 *Case of the Lecturer of St. Anne's Westminster*, 2 Stra. 1192 (1743), also reported sub nom. *The King v. Bishop of London*, 1 Wils. K.B. 11.

Bench can decide all questions of law concerning them. In fact, the court never hesitated to decide what was sufficient cause for removal from office, although its reasons for claiming this power are conspicuously missing from the reports.

The relationship of King's Bench to "inferior jurisdictions" as developed up to about 1700 was expounded by Chief Justice Hardwicke with textbook clarity, in a decision which, like many such textbook decisions, was not laid down until its doctrine was a little out of date. In *The King v. the Bishop of Litchfield* (1734)[34] an alternative mandamus issued to the bishop to license one Rushworth as a school teacher in a free grammar school, following his election by the inhabitants of the city. Lord Hardwicke said:

> I make no doubt but that the ordinary has power of judging the person [when he licenses schoolmasters] but it is very material whether that is founded on canon law, or any implied authority by the several acts of Parliament. If the first, this Court has nothing to do in it, but the party must take his remedy by appeal to some superior ecclesiastical court; but if he derive his power from the temporal law, he must proceed according to the limitations annexed to it; and we are judges whether that power is properly executed or not.

The College Cases

In the great college cases of the Restoration and post-Restoration periods, in which the court was asked to restore a number of fellows to their academic positions, the analogy of mandamus to prohibition was extended still farther. These cases were found particularly difficult to decide because it was not clear whether colleges were

34 7 Mod. 217, 219.

lay foundations subject to the common law or spiritual foundations ruled by canon law—the question on which debate centered at first. Another line of reasoning was developed: whether lay or spiritual, the duly appointed visitor of a college "has a jurisdiction" as to questions grounded on the college statutes, and no mandamus will go on such questions. That is, a respondent agency or court may have an area of discretion even though it is not based on the spiritual law. From this position it is only a short jump to the modern notion that even an agency whose powers are conferred by statute may have discretion in some matters.

The problem of the colleges was first posed in *Dr. Widdrington's Case.* Dr. Widdrington sought to be restored to his fellowship at Christ's College, Cambridge (he had been appointed as regius professor by Oliver Cromwell in 1654, and was removed by his colleagues on the Restoration). An alternative mandamus issued. The college returned the power of the master and dean to correct any peccant fellow, "and if he find himself aggrieved with his punishment, it is lawful for him to appeal to the chancellor of the University, and two senior doctors." The court held that this return was sufficient, and that the doctor ought to resort to the visitors named therein, "for, by *Wyndham* (J.) of every hospital or eleemosynary foundation, appeal ought to be made to the visitors, for they have the supervising of all things concerning them; and if they have no visitors, then the ordinary, vide *Lindwood,* tit. *de Religiosis Domibus* . . . and everyone ought to appeal to the next Court, Fitzherb., Error 87."[35]

[35] T. Raym. 31; also 1 Lev. 23, 1 Keb. 2, 131 (Pasch. and Mich., 13 Car. 2, 1661).

The second college case was argued at great length and the court, being equally divided, was unable to decide it.[36] Dr. Patrick, a moderate royalist, had been duly elected in 1662 to the mastership of Queen's College, Cambridge, but the senior fellow was "of the party of another who stood in competition with Dr. Patrick" and refused to admit and swear him. Probably the fact that King Charles II had ordered the fellows to elect that other (one Anthony Sparrow, a high churchman) had had something to do with the senior fellow's refusal. Ten years later Charles made it up to Dr. Patrick by appointing him a royal chaplain "whether he would or no."

Queen's College was founded by Queen Margaret, wife of King Henry VI, and no visitor was named in the college charter. By a letter patent of James I, confirming the statutes of all colleges in the universities, it was provided that where no special visitor was named for a college, the university chancellor should be visitor if he was present and the vice-chancellor in his absence, provided that the vice-chancellor had been duly deputized and appointed. At the time of Dr. Patrick's election the chancellor was absent, but the vice-chancellor had not been specifically appointed visitor.

Both parties and three of the four judges in the case seem to have agreed that if there was a visitor at the relevant time, mandamus ought not to go. The college's main argument was that Patrick had made no appeal, that an appeal lay to the Bishop of Ely as ordinary because the college was a spiritual foundation, and so the bishop was visitor. As a makeweight, counsel added that even if the college were temporal it was a private society whose

36 *Dr. Patrick's Case,* 1 Lev. 65; T. Raym. 101; 1 Keb. 289, 294, 298, 551, 610, 665; 2 Keb. 65, 164, 259 (1662-68).

affairs did not concern the public. But the fourth judge, Justice Moreton, thought that mandamus ought to go even though the college was a spiritual corporation, because the master of a college has a freehold which the ordinary as visitor cannot try: "the college may be ecclesiastical and yet the head be lay." The ordinary's power "extended not to try this freehold, which is temporal."[37] Justice Keeling (who at an earlier stage of the case had been of counsel for Dr. Patrick) agreed with Moreton that Patrick had a freehold. He thought that the college was a lay corporation with no certain visitor at the relevant time. Therefore mandamus ought to go, because "there is great mischief to leave an uncontroulable power in any person or persons whatever to doe wrong, as here would be, if remedy be not applied by this mandatory writ."[38] This same Justice Kelyng or Keeling seems not to have seen any "great mischief" in "an uncontroulable power" in himself. His bearing on the bench "was haughty and brutal, and he did not scruple to browbeat, fine, and even imprison the jury." The House of Commons investigated the charge and resolved that such proceedings were illegal, but proceeded no further.[39]

Justices Windham and Twisden both thought that no mandamus should go for Dr. Patrick. Twisden thought that the college was a lay foundation and so by the common law the founder's heir—that is, the King—was visitor.[40] Windham thought that it was immaterial whether the college was lay or spiritual. Mandamus ought not to go:

37 2 Keb. 164, 165.

38 2 Keb. 172.

39 *Dict. Nat. Biog.*, article "Kelyng, Sir John."

40 The special facts of this case then raised the fascinating question whether visitatorial power could pass by escheat, for the bodily heirs of the founder, Queen Margaret, had been killed in the Wars of the Roses.

The question will be, whether on a controversy . . . which is grounded on the Statute of the College and customs of the University, this Court may award a *Mandamus* to try it, and I hold no *Mandamus* ought to have been granted . . . for the Court *ex officio* do take notice of the privileges of the Universities . . . on motion for *Mandamus* in times best adorned with learning, that they must proceed *secundum morem universitatis,* which is either by the Founders or Chancellors of the university, and this Court takes notice of the jurisdiction of the five Ports, County Palatine, etc., much rather shall they take notice of the University, which gives us light . . . and to judge in these Courts according to the laws and foundations of another's Conusance, as whether each has done his Exercise well, this will tend to dissolve the University, and much trouble *Westminster Hall,* and it's an inconvenience on both hands.[41]

In other words, (1) whether lay or spiritual, the college authorities "have a jurisdiction" based on the founder's grant and statutes, and (2) it would be bad policy and inconvenient for King's Bench to intervene in the affairs of colleges.

During the next few years it was made clear that the significance of an appeal to the visitor was not merely procedural—not, so to speak, a matter of exhaustion of administrative remedies—as had been suggested in *Dr. Widdrington.* In *Dr. Robert's Case*[42] mandamus was refused on an affidavit that the relator had applied to the visitor for redress "and he would not meddle," and in *Daniel Appleford's Case*[43] the visitor had affirmed the action of the college.

But it seems that mandamus would go where the law of the land, or the rights of one outside the university

41 2 Keb. 166.
42 2 Keb. 102 (Mich., 18 Car. 2, 1666).
43 1 Mod. 82, 2 Lev. 14, 2 Keb. 799, 861 (23 & 24 Car. 2, 1671 and 1672).

community and so not subject to the visitor, were concerned. In *The King v. St. John's College, Cambridge*[44] the Crown asked a mandamus to require the college to expel certain fellows who were "nonjurors," that is, had refused to swear allegiance to William III after the Revolution of 1688, as required by statute. The court (Chief Justice Holt, according to gossip in later cases) said: "The Visitor is made by *the founder,* and is the proper judge of the private laws of the college; he is to determine offences against those laws. But where the law of the land is disobeyed, this court will take notice thereof notwithstanding *the Visitor*; and in this case the proper way to put it in execution is by this writ of *mandamus.*" In the particular case, however, the writ was denied because the fellows to be removed were not parties to the proceedings.

Two terms later one King sought a mandamus against St. John's College, Oxford. King had been nominated by the City of Bristol, under a provision of the college charter that two scholars of the college should always be so chosen. The college returned to the alternative mandamus that the Bishop of Winchester was its visitor, and that they had refused to admit King because he was "incapable of the scholarship." Chief Justice Holt said: "The Visitor shall determine all, that relates to Persons that are of the Foundation; but here is a collateral Interest in Bristol, they are no Part of the College, the Visitor hath no Power before a Person be made a Member."[45] The report does not indicate whether a peremptory mandamus issued in this case. But in 1764 a peremptory

44 Skinner 359, 4 Mod. 233 at 241 (Mich., 5 W. & M., 1693).

45 *Rex et Reg. v. St. John's College,* Oxon., Comb. 238, also reported 4 Mod. 260, 368 (5 & 6 W. & M., 1695 and 1696).

mandamus went to the University of Cambridge to set its seal to the appointment of Lord Hardwicke as high steward.[46]

To summarize: As to questions "grounded on the college statutes" an alternative mandamus will go; but if the college returns that has a visitor, no peremptory mandamus will go. It is immaterial whether the college be considered as lay or spiritual, for the visitor "has a jurisdiction" in these matters in any case. The single exception is that mandamus will go to protect the rights of one outside the college community, over whom the visitor has no power, even though his claim is founded on the college statutes. *Parkinson's Case* (1689) gives two reasons for this treatment of colleges: "because those are private Foundations, and governed by particular Laws of the Founders, for which Reason this Court cannot take notice of their private Ordinances. Besides, every Fellow of a College when he is admitted to a Fellowship, he accepts it under such a Condition, that he shall submit to the Government of the Visitor of that College."[47] As to questions grounded on Acts of Parliament, mandamus will issue to colleges as to other corporations. The argument that the fellow of a college has a freehold is not in itself sufficient to bring King's Bench in, perhaps because he does not have a freehold, but no reason for this rule was ever given.

Thus stated, the analogy to the law of prohibition is close, with the college statutes treated as analogous to the ecclesiastical laws. With one exception, this series of cases is the first in which it is recognized that temporal authorities as well as spiritual may "have a jurisdiction."

[46] *The King v. University of Cambridge*, 1 W. Bl. 547 (1764).
[47] Carthew 92, 3 Mod. 265 (Mich., 1 W. & M., 1689).

It is also the series in which this principle is carried furthest. This was at least in part because King's Bench did not wish to decide "whether each has done his Exercise well"[48] or like questions.

Prin's Case[49] is the earliest mandamus recognizing an area of temporal law in which the respondent is free from control by King's Bench and this administrative discretion is directly conferred by statute. Prin was turned out of the recordership of Bath by the commissioners of corporations (the Restoration equivalent of a loyalty board for municipal officers), under the statute 13 Charles 2, stat. 2, c. 1. An alternative mandamus issued to restore him, but the court privately advised the commissioners that "their return would be sufficient, if only that they thought it expedient." The statute gave the commissioners full power to proceed if they "deem it expedient for the public safety."

The commissioners might well have had difficulty in expressing their reasons for ousting Prin. For this was William Prynne, the Puritan lawyer-pamphleteer who had had his ears cropped on the pillory three separate times under Charles I for libeling Archbishop Laud and the bishops. Later he conducted Laud's prosecution before the Long Parliament. But as the Civil Wars progressed Prynne, an Erastian Presbyterian in theory, and by temperament a natural "againster," attacked nearly everyone —the Independents, the Scottish Presbyterians, and Cromwell's army. He was purged from the Parliament by Colonel Pride in 1648 and proceeded to attack the Rump. But when the King was executed he turned Royalist, had

48 *Dr. Patrick's Case*, 2 Keb. 166.

49 1 Keb. 520, 686 (15 & 16 Car. 2, 1663-64). Justices Heath and Mallet had of course recognized this possibility on review by certiorari so early as *Commins v. Massam* (1642).

some share in a plot of 1650 to restore Charles II, and was imprisoned by the Council of State for three years. Next he attacked the Barebones Parliament, Cromwell, and the Protectorate, and took some part in a Royalist rising of 1658.

In 1659 Prynne sat in Parliament for one day, claiming his right to sit despite his exclusion in 1648. When General Monk marched south from Scotland the "secluded members" were at last readmitted to the Parliament, on Monk's order. Prynne led the way, with a basket-hilt sword "longer than ordinary" at his side which tripped up another Member of Parliament. Then he pamphleteered for a restoration of the King and was elected to the Convention Parliament of 1660. But no sooner were King and bishops restored than Prynne returned to his old sport of attacking the bishops—though not the King. At this juncture came his removal from the recordership of Bath; yet he was re-elected to Parliament over the court party's opposition, and lived to a ripe though not a tranquil old age.

Significantly, other cases recognizing that discretion or "jurisdiction" may be derived from statute or temporal law do not appear until considerably later. Although mandamus will lie to justices of sessions to compel them to hear an appeal, it will not lie in such a case if the appeal was denied because a rule of practice in the sessions had not been complied with. The sessions "are the properest judges of practice at the sessions, and all courts must have stated rules to go by."[50] Nor will it lie to require justices of peace to license a named person to keep an alehouse,[51] nor to assign the assets of a bank-

50 *Anon.*, 1 Stra. 315 (1720).
51 *Anon.*, 1 Barnard. K.B. 402 (1730).

rupt to a named creditor.[52] Mandamus lies to parish authorities or justices of peace "to make an equal rate for the poor" where they have made no rate at all, but King's Bench will not intervene merely because an existing rate is said to be unequal,[53] nor on suggestion that some people have been improperly left out of a poor rate (and thereby deprived of their votes for member of Parliament). "This court never went further, than to oblige the making of a rate, without meddling with the question, who is to be put in or left out; of which the parish officers are the proper judges subject to an appeal [to sessions]."[54]

In the first quarter of the eighteenth century it could not yet be said that the law of mandamus was a coherent whole. We have seen that each new application, as it was made, was governed by reasoning analogous to that used in the law of prohibition. But each such application led to a line of precedents that was felt as separate, on the whole, and the separate lines of precent developed side by side—freehold, restoration to various offices, enforcement of certain statutes, the college cases, and the like. The emphasis of the cases is on precedent. No comprehensive theory of mandamus was articulated until Lord Mansfield's familiar judgment in *Rex v. Barker*,[55] the lead-

52 *R. v. Justices of Surrey*, 2 Barnard. K.B. 410 (1734).

53 *Dr. Butler v. Cobbett*, 11 Mod. 255 (1709); *The King v. Inhabitants of Barnstable*, 1 Barnard. K.B. 137 (1728); *The King v. Churchwardens of the Parish of Wilkinton*, 1 Barnard. K.B. 227 (1729).

54 *Dom. Rex v. Churchwardens of Weobly*, 2 Stra. 1259 (1746). *Ashby v. White*, 1 Salk. 19, 3 Salk. 17, 2 Ld. Raym. 938 (1703), suggests the possibility of a different argument in this case.

55 3 Burr. 1265 (1762). Serjeant Glyn in *Estwick v. City of London*, Style 32 at 42 (1647) was concerned with "the very nature of the writ of Restitution," an earlier and narrower thing.

ing case in modern law. The language of *Amherst's Case*[56] may be a beginning toward such a theory: "this Court will interpose when any Officers will not do Justice, or will outgo their Authority: For there is the same reason to command to do Justice, as to prohibit Injustice." But by itself the meaning of "justice" is a little too vague for legal reasoning. Something a little more precise was foreshadowed in *Peat's Case*,[57] denying the writ because "a *mandamus* is always to do some act in execution of law."

But probably the idea of mandamus as a means of enforcing legal rights generally was simply too broad and indefinite for the legal mind to accept until some ascertainable limits on it had been set. Otherwise, what was to stop it from displacing the whole revered structure of common-law remedies? An appropriate limit was eventually found precisely in the rule that mandamus would not lie where the relator had another legal remedy. So formulated, this rule appears without ambiguity only so late as 1737, when a mandamus to rerate a taxpayer was denied because, as Chief Justice Lee said, "the party is not without remedy. For she may bring an appeal."[58] The converse proposition—that mandamus ought to go because otherwise the relator will have no remedy—was often argued by seventeenth century counsel; but it seems to have been more an appeal to the judges' general sense of justice than to any specific legal principle. Thus Serjeant Bartholomew Shower in *Dom. Rex v. Oxenden:* "here's a man injured; there's no relief in the world but submission to the wrongdoer, unless you allow him the

56 1 Ventr. 187; also reported T. Raym. 214 (Hil., 23-24 Car. 2, 1671/72).
57 6 Mod. 228 (1704).
58 *The King v. Churchwardens, etc., of Freshford,* Andrews 24.

aid of this writ."[59]

Lord Mansfield's generalization in *Rex v. Blooer*[60] —"A *mandamus to restore* is the true Specific Remedy where a person is wrongfully dispossessed of any Office or Function which draws after it Temporal Rights, in all cases where the established Course of Law has not provided a *Specific* Remedy by another form of proceeding" —contained not only sound legal scholarship but creative force for the future. The pattern was in the cases, but it was overlaid with unnecessary complications; it took Lord Mansfield's insight to see its fundamental simplicity. In the same way, in *Rex v. Barker*[61] he said "A *Mandamus* . . . was introduced, to prevent Disorder from a Failure of Justice and defect of Police. Therefore it ought to be used upon all Occasions where the Law has established no Specific Remedy, and where in Justice and good Government there *ought* to be one . . . If there be a right, and *no other* Specific Remedy, *This* should not be denied."

59 1 Show. K.B. 217 at 218 (Trin., 3 W. & M., 1691).
60 2 Burr. 1043 at 1045 (1760).
61 3 Burr. 1265 at 1267 (1762).

V

JURISDICTION AND LEGALITY: CERTIORARI

THERE ARE many oddities in the history of law, but nothing odder than the fact that so much of the early development of modern administrative law is to be found in the cases on the poor law. To be sure, this was an area where the impact of the law was sharply felt and the citizen needed protection. But in general the courts did not intervene to protect the poor person, who could be shipped from one parish to another for no offense except that of being poor, with or without his children, and without a thought of his consent. They intervened usually to arbitrate between parishes anxious to escape the cost and responsibility of providing for their poor. Both courts and litigants would have been astonished to see what later periods have built on that foundation. Yet the notions of administrative discretion and of a limited but definite scope of judicial review, fundamental to the rule of law in the complexities of modern society, do nevertheless begin there.

We have shown that the subspecies certiorari to quash evolved from the medieval certiorari for removal by several steps. First the writ became available to remove orders of justices of peace and of sewers commissioners (as well as presentments and indictments before them), for trial in King's Bench. Then the trial at bar was eliminated, leaving only a motion to quash the order.

It is most probable that the theory of the proper scope of review by King's Bench, as articulated in the eighteenth century and still current, derives indirectly from that historical process. In fact, attention was first drawn to that development by the close correspondence of the eighteenth-century pattern of review to the issues that would naturally be before the court at the outset of a removal proceeding. It will be convenient at this point to state the eighteenth-century doctrine.

On certiorari, an order would be quashed if the justices had no jurisdiction to make it; and "nothing is presumed in a limited jurisdiction."[1] Every "point of jurisdiction" was required to be fully set forth in the order, and no inferences from its language were permissible.[2] Moreover, even when on the face of an order the jurisdiction was fully made out, affidavit evidence could be used to show that in fact the justices did not have jurisdiction.[3] But *nothing else* need be set forth, "there is no Necessity for setting out the Reason of their Judgment: We never do it in this Court."[4]

If, however, the justices chose to give reasons for their order, the reasons must be sufficient,[5] at least where it

1 *Dom. Rex v. Inhabitantes of Almanbury,* 1 Stra. 96 (1718).

2 *The King v. Childers,* 1 Barnard. K.B. 326 (1730); *The King v. Inhabitants of Woodsterton,* 2 Barnard. K.B. 207, 247 (1732-33); *Dom. Rex v. Inhabitants of Brackley,* Cunningham 80 (1734).

3 *The King v. Bowden* or *Bolton,* 2 Barnard. K.B. 144 and 149 (1732).

4 *The King v. Inhabitants of Ripon,* 2 W. Kelyng 295, 2 Barnard. K.B. 372 (1733).

5 *Parish of St. Alban's v. Parish of St. Botolph's Bishop's Gate,* 11 Mod. 205 (1708/09).

appeared that they had stated the case fully. Clearly the reasons given must not conclude against their order, but an order stating the facts specially might perhaps still be good where it appeared that they had merely omitted to state some part of their reasons. Thus a married woman, whose settlement ordinarily depended on her husband's, could be sent to her own last legal settlement unless it was expressly stated in the order that her husband had a different settlement.[6] The justices' general conclusions of fact, following the language of the statute, must be adjudicated by some such phrase as "it appears to us" and must not be merely a recital of the evidence.[7] But no error of law that did not appear "on the face of the record" could be excepted to in King's Bench (unless it was a "jurisdictional matter").[8] Even a bill of exceptions sealed by the justices below would not serve to bring error not "on the face" before King's Bench.[9] This is even now the theoretical pattern for review on certiorari.

When this much has been said, however, the more difficult question remains: what points "go to the jurisdiction" and so must be stated for the order to be valid; and what points are merely "reasons for their judgment," need not be stated, and cannot be reviewed unless stated. It is this question that makes clear the salient difference between the seventeenth century and later times.

It is extremely difficult to trace a pattern of review from the seventeenth-century cases, for the reports often give no reason at all for a decision and usually do not

6 *Dunsfold Inhabitants v. Dunsfold Windsborough Green Inhabitants,* Gilb. Cas. 97 (1713); *The King v. Gayer,* 1 Ld. Ken. 492 (1757).

7 *The Queen v. The Parish of Kidderminster,* 11 Mod. 265 (1709).

8 *The King v. The Inhabitants of Drakemast,* 2 Barnard. K.B. 99 (1731). *The King v. Inhabitants of Oulton,* Cas. t. Hardw. 159 (1735).

9 *The King v. Inhabitants of Preston-on-the-Hill,* 2 Stra. 1040 (1736).

recite the language of the order being reviewed. But the germ of the eighteenth-century rules and of their application seems to lie in Sir Robert Heath's remarkable opinion in *Commins v. Massam*, in which he argued that the proceedings of sewers commissioners are reviewable in King's Bench, but the scope of that review must be limited:

No ordinary Judges in the realm have this power; but this Court is *Coram Rege ipso*, and notwithstanding that the act leaves the proceedings to the discretion of the Commissioners, nevertheless this discretion is examinable and controllable in this Court. Suppose that the Commissioners do anything without or against their Commission, without doubt this is reformable and examinable here: But as for Courts of Aequity, as of the Marches of Wales and the like, this Court cannot take notice whether their decrees are just or not: We are alone to examine their *Jurisdiction of the case, not their Justice*. They themselves are to answer for that, as we for the law: Let us put the case that A bargains and sells to B, and C gives collateral security to B: and the Commissioners make a decree against C, this is against the law, and therefore reformable by us, but equitable cases are nothing to us.

Heath then discussed a number of arguments against the decree in *Commins v. Massam:* The commissioners have power by the statute to tax owners and occupiers; but is the executor of a lessee an occupier within the statute? An executor is not charged with the liabilities of his testator unless he has assets; but it does not appear that the defendant had assets. Can the commissioners properly take notice of the lessee's covenant to pay for all repairs to the premises? He found that none of these objections were well founded, and concluded: "This court has jurisdiction of the decree of the Commissioners if it is illegal: but in the case at bar there is no injustice, their commission was well executed: and if the party conceives himself oppressed, he should repair to the Chancery to have more Equity."[10]

It is to be noted that Justice Heath discusses review of the commissioner's jurisdiction and review of the legality of their order in the same breath. Further, the arguments of law that he considers are based both on the Statute of Sewers and on the common law. Thus it seems that the meaning of "jurisdiction" in these cases was never thought through in the seventeenth century. By the time the surface logic of the present rules of review had been formulated, in the 1730's, there were ninety years' accumulated precedents which could not be reconciled with those rules except by verbal juggling; and the juggling has continued ever since.

One decisive set of facts emerges from the seventeenth-century precedents: There is *no case* in the reports before 1695 in which King's Bench refused to review an objection based on the language of the applicable statute, whether or not the objection is properly "jurisdictional," and whether or not the objection appears "on the face" of the order. Many orders, on the other hand, were quashed because "it does not appear" that a statutory requirement had been followed, whether or not that requirement was properly jurisdictional by modern criteria.

Yet it is probable that the "face of the record" rule existed. Such a rule would be appropriate to a preliminary motion to quash, for questions of fact or errors of law not on the face could be raised later on if the motion to quash was lost. There would be no need to raise

10 Harvard Law School (Turner) MS 113, pp. 171, 173.

them at this preliminary stage and in fact, since they need proofs outside the record, they would be better left until the facts can be properly offered in evidence.

The rule is strongly suggested in one case of 1661/62, *The King v. The Churchwardens of C.* An order of sessions concerning poor relief was challenged, on the ground (it appears) that it was made in a later year to reimburse an overseer who had spent money for the poor out of his own pocket. Justice Foster raised the further objection: "he disbursing without consent of his Partners and no care being taken Monthly for to take Accompts, this Order is null. [Justice] Windham contra, that the Order being good of itself, the Court will not quash it for matter dehors suggested."[11]

In *Wooton Rivers v. St. Peter's Marlborough* (1695)[12] a reverse aspect of the "face of the record" rule was stated and applied. A missing point of jurisdiction was sought to be supplied from a statement in the justices' return to the certiorari, but Chief Justice Holt said: "though upon the return of the *certiorari* 'tis set forth that this order is made *upon the complaint of the churchwardens and overseers of the poor,* yet that will not supply the omission in the order itself . . . they had no power to make such a return; they should only have returned the order *in haec verba.*"

The argument made in *The Queen v. London* (1704),[13] noted below, implies the existence of the "face of the

11 1 Keb. 236 (Hil., 13 Car. 2, 1661/62). There was no requirement in the statutes that the overseers keep monthly accounts. It does require them to meet monthly and to render an account to the two next justices of peace at the end of the year, from which a requirement of monthly accounts might be implied.

12 3 Salk. 254, 5 Mod. 149 (Hil., 7 Will. 3, 1695/96).

13 6 Mod. 204.

record" rule at that date. Again, in a case of 1718, a particularly unfair argument was based on the rule. By the statute 13 & 14 Charles 2, c. 12, the justices could remove poor persons likely to become chargeable to the parish to their last legal settlements. But also by the statute a poor person might bring a certificate from the churchwardens and overseers of his legal settlement, acknowledging their responsibility for him, if he wished to move to another parish, and then he was not to be sent back before he was actually chargeable. One Abraham Hatchett was removed as "likely to become chargeable" by an order that did not mention the fact that he was a certificate-man; and it was argued that this point could not be raised since it did not appear "on the face." The court seems to have agreed with this argument, but quashed the order on other grounds.[14] Thereafter the rule seems to have been taken for granted.

Nevertheless, it was not until 1732 that the "face of the record" rule was applied squarely so as to allow the justices to ignore a statutory requirement. In *The King v. Inhabitants of Woodsterton*[15] the statute required a summons, but an order that mentioned none was confirmed. Then began the attempts by complainants with good objections in law to evade the rule—attempts which continued until the Tribunals and Inquiries Act, 1958.[16]

In *The King v. The Inhabitants of Hornbey*[17] counsel for the parish were given leave to apply to the justices of sessions to amend their return, for "they observed, that the Truth of the Fact was with them, and appeared so to

14 *Parish of Burclear v. Parish of Eastwoodhay*, 1 Stra. 163.

15 *The King v. Inhabitants of Woodsterton*, 2 Barnard. K.B. 207, 247.

16 6 & 7 Eliz. 2, c. 66.

17 2 Barnard. K.B. 115 (1731/32).

the Justices of the Sessions, though the Justices have not stated the Fact so upon their Order." In *The King v. Inhabitants of Sympson*[18] and *The King v. Reading*[19] the effect of the rule was worked out in great detail for the case when a general order of justices was followed by a special order of sessions or vice versa. In the mid-thirties another attempt was made to avoid the rule by means of a bill of exceptions, but Lord Hardwicke held reluctantly[20] that no bill of exceptions would lie for orders of justices.

But in spite of the probability that the "face of the record" rule already existed, the fundamental fact is that before 1695 the court never once refused to review an objection based on applicable statutory language. Every such question was decided on the merits, whether the objection was based on the language of the order or on an omission from the order. There are many cases quashing an order because "it does not appear" that a statutory requirement was complied with. Sometimes the missing factor in these cases is jurisdictional in the proper sense of the word, that is, necessary to show that the justices had power to entertain the case at all.[21] More often it is not: many of these cases involve procedural steps of all kinds, or findings of fact. There are eighteenth-century cases labeling many of these missing statutory factors as "jurisdictional"; and it is suggested that the seventeenth century considered every statutory requirement as a matter of jurisdiction, in some sense. It is not possible

18 1 Barnard. K.B. 435 (1731).

19 Cas. t. Hardw. 73 (1734).

20 *The King v. Inhabitants of Preston-on-the-Hill*, Cas. t. Hardw. 236 (1736).

21 *Anonymous*, Style 14 (Pasch., 23 Car., 1647). Cf. also *The King v. Apsley*, Style 85 (Hil., 23 Car., 1647/48).

otherwise to reconcile the results of the cases with the evidence that a "face of the record" rule existed. Moreover, there is language in some of the cases to support this suggestion.

Orders were quashed because facts had not been found, as follows:

On an order that one parish should distribute to the poor of another in a different hundred, because there was no finding that no other parish within the hundred was able to do so.[22]

On an order of sewers to build a ditch for flood control, no finding that the parties ordered to do so were damaged by the floods.[23]

On an order for payment of a servant's wages, no finding that the servant was hired according to the applicable statute.[24]

On poor-law removal orders, no finding that the poor person was likely to become chargeable to the parish,[25] or that the place to which he was removed was his last legal settlement.[26]

On an order that a father-in-law should support his son's widow, no finding that he was financially able to do so.[27]

But the first case in which such a finding of fact was clearly labeled as "jurisdictional" was *The King v. Gully* (1715). An order of sessions that a father should contribute to his daughter's maintenance was quashed "because it

22 *Anonymous*, 1 Keb. 685 (Hil., 15 & 16 Car. 2, 1663/64).

23 *The King v. Wright*, 2 Keb. 42 (Pasch., 18 Car. 2, 1666).

24 *Snape v. Dowse*, Comb. 3 (Mich., 1 Jac. 2, 1685).

25 *The Queen v. Inhabitants of Newnham Murrey*, 6 Mod. 163 (1704).

26 *Inhabitants of Berry v. Inhabitants of Arundel*, 2 Salk. 479 (Pasch., 9 Will. 3, 1697).

27 *The Queen v. Dunn*, 10 Mod. 221 (1714).

was not set forth in the order that she was unable to work, without which the justices have no jurisdiction. But by unable to work, the act means a person not able by work to get his own living, and not a person that is able to get nothing at all."[28] In *Inhabitants of King's Langley*,[29] an order to remove a poor child to its birthplace was quashed for lack of a statement that the justices could not find the father's settlement, "for this gives them jurisdiction."

The first case in which the "face of the record" rule was said to apply to a statutory requirement was of this type. In *Wooton Rivers v. St. Peter's Marlborough* it was objected that an order of two justices for removing a poor woman to her legal settlement did not state that she did not rent a tenement worth ten pounds per annum. The statute, 13 & 14 Charles 2, c. 12, empowered justices of peace to make such removal orders "within fourty days after any such person or persons coming to settle . . . in any tenement under the yearly value of Ten pounds." The omission in the order obviously worried Chief Justice Holt, but he said that the justices had power to make removal orders before the statute, and

> since the power to remove a poor person being not wholly founded on the statute 13 & 14 Car. 2, but on the law as it was before the making that statute, whether such an order as would serve for a removal before that statute, would serve since, or whether the statute obliges the justices to alter the form of their orders; *and this depends on the operation of the statute, whether it was by way of jurisdiction or restriction;* and upon searching of precedents by the secondary he found, that the orders before this statute were all without this clause, and so were the orders since; whereupon, as to this point, this

28 10 Mod. 307.
29 Fort. 323 (1724).

order was held good; and if the fact is, that the person removed *doth rent a tenement* of 10 £ per annum, it ought to be remedied by way of appeal to the sessions.[30]

Even this case falls short of a square holding that a statutory requirement can be left out of an order, since the order was quashed on other grounds. It is unfortunate that the italicized passage is so cryptic; is Lord Holt saying that every requirement of a statute that operates "by way of jurisdiction" must appear in an order based thereon, but not the requirements of a statute that operates "by way of restriction"? The passage does show, however, that he thought of the problem as one of jurisdiction in some way.

Failure to state statutory procedural steps was also sometimes treated as "jurisdictional." For instance, orders were quashed for these reasons:

On a poor-law removal, for failure to state that complaint had been made by the churchwardens and overseers of the poor,[31] for failure to state that one of the two justices acting was of the quorum as required by statute,[32] and for failure to state that the order was made at the quarter sessions and not merely at the general sessions, when the statute so requires.[33]

On an order to pay a surgeon for treating a poor patient, for failure to state that the churchwardens and overseers had employed the surgeon.[34]

30 3 Salk. 254, 5 Mod. 149 (Hil., 7 Will. 3, 1695/96). Italics mine.

31 *Wooton Rivers v. St. Peter's Marlborough*, and *The King v. Inhabitants of Hareby*, Andrews 361 (1738).

32 *Inter Inhabitant' Chittinston and Penshurst*, 2 Salk. 473, 475 (Mich., 8 Will. 3, 1696).

33 *King v. Turner*, 5 Mod. 329 (Hil., 8 Will. 3, 1696/97).

34 *Inhabitants of St. Paul v. Faringdon*, Fort. 313 (1708).

On an order for payment of tithes, for failure to state that a special statutory procedure had been followed.[35]

On an order of sessions confirming the accounts of overseers of the poor, for failure to state that the accounts had been approved by the two next justices.[36]

The language of some cases shows fairly clearly that for the seventeenth and eighteenth centuries the "jurisdiction" of an inferior court included its statutory authority. In *Ball v. Pattridge*[37] certiorari was asked to remove the proceedings of the commissioners of the fens, whose function was to determine rival claims to lands in the newly drained Great Level. Some of the claimants claimed through the Duke of Bedford and his associates in the draining project, and others were "squatters" of long standing. The court said:

> This is a new and absolute Judicature in the Commissioners by this new Law with which this Court has nothing to do if they proceed according to the Statute for then this obliges perpetually. But if they do not proceed according to the Statute when everything is void, and *coram non judice,* and the parties are free to examine this in an action brought at the common law.

In *Inhabitants of Chittinston v. Inhabitants of Penshurst* the court said that justices of peace "have a special jurisdiction given by the Act, which must be followed."[38] In *The King v. The Townships of Waldersham, etc.,* in 1718, Chief Justice Pratt and Justices Powys and Eyre are reported as saying that in the order in controversy, "The justices assume an original authority which they

35 *The King v. Bowden,* 2 Barnard. K.B. 144 (1732).

36 *Dom. Rex v. Bartlett,* 2 Stra. 983 (1733).

37 1 Sid. 296 (Trin., 18 Car. 2, 1666).

38 5 Mod. 321.

have not." Chief Justice Fortescue adds immediately, "The order is void for the generality, if they had a jurisdiction," and the order is quashed.[39] In *The Queen v. Dunn*,[40] *The King v. Sheringbrook*,[41] and *The King v. Occupiers of Land in Burough-Fen*[42] orders are quashed simply for noncompliance with statutory requirements, without express reference to the notion of jurisdiction, but with language which is at least suggestive.

The uncertain relationship between statutes and jurisdiction in the eighteenth century is most clearly illustrated by a group of cases on the question whether a summons to the defendant is necessary in varying circumstances. This is a point which would certainly be classified as jurisdictional in modern law, yet the eighteenth century cases require that a summons be set forth only when the applicable statute calls for it. In paternity orders, the whole court agreed that natural justice requires that the defendant be summoned, but the judges were evenly divided as to whether a summons must be set forth in the order.[43] There is no provision for summons in the applicable statute 18 Elizabeth, c. 3. In *The King v. Venables*[44] it was held that no summons need be set forth in an order of sessions to suppress an alehouse; although a summons is legally necessary and a criminal information will lie against the justices for proceeding without one. Again there is no statutory provision for a summons. But an order discharging an apprentice was

39 11 Mod. 280.
40 10 Mod. 221 (1714) "in which case only the act enables the justices."
41 2 Ld. Raym. 1394 (1724) "which is expressly required by the words of the act."
42 1 Barnard. K.B. 2 (1726) "*non constat* that they have pursued the authority given them by the statute."
43 *Dom. Rex v. Cleg*, 1 Stra. 475, 8 Mod. 4 (1721).
44 2 Ld. Raym. 1405 (1725).

quashed "because it does not appear the master was present or summoned, which it is plain the act intended he should be."[45]

In many cases orders were quashed because the remedy ordered was improper according to the statutes, and their language sometimes suggests that this is a matter of jurisdiction. "The justices had no power by the statute" to order the reputed father of an illegitimate child to pay for his maintenance "until further order."[46] "The justices cannot" suppress an alehouse once duly licensed except for disorder.[47] An order that the mother's employer should pay half the cost of maintaining a bastard child because the employer had connived at the parents' misbehavior, was quashed because "this was not within the statute";[48] similarly an order discharging an apprentice on his own request was attacked as "not warranted by the statute," but was confirmed.[49] An order of sewers "for the straitning of the public stream, whereby the meadows of A. and B. could not be overflowed as usual" received the court's comment: "the Commissioners cannot meddle with it, unless it be a publick prejudice as well as a publick stream."[50]

In *The Queen v. London* (1704)[51] the justices made an order for payment of a laborer's wages for work in the King's garden at Hampton Court, stating these facts

[45] *Dominus Rex v. Easman,* 2 Stra. 1013 (1735). The act, 5 Eliz., c. 4, empowers the justices to take action "upon his [the master's] appearance and hearing of the matter."

[46] *Dom. Rex v. Thomas,* 2 Show. K.B. 129 (Mich., 32 Car. 2, 1680).

[47] *Dom. Rex v. Randall,* 2 Salk. 470 (Mich., 7 Will. 3, 1695).

[48] *Anonymous,* Style 207 (Hil. 1649/50).

[49] *Hawkesworth and Hillary's Case,* 1 Saund. 314 (Mich., 21 Car. 2, 1669).

[50] *Dom. Rex v. Vachel,* 3 Keb. 446 (Pasch., 27 Car. 2, 1675).

[51] 6 Mod. 204 (1704).

specially. The order was quashed for error on its face, since the statute only gives the justices power over wages in husbandry. Counsel's somewhat confused argument, however, clearly conceived this as a matter of jurisdiction:

If the order had been generally for *wages,* there the Court would not intend it to be other than *wages in husbandry,* and it might hold; but where on the face of the order it appears otherwise . . . it is in itself void, as touching a matter whereof they have no jurisdiction. . . . Then this is a question of jurisdiction, and acts of parliament concerning jurisdiction ought to be taken strictly, and all the matter of equity that may be urged on the other side is shut out by this one answer, that it is against a positive law.

The truth of the matter appears to be that it was not until about 1720 that the notion of jurisdiction was fully separated from that of statutory authority, that is, that the doctrine became clear that not every requirement of statute need be treated as jurisdictional. The distinction was implicit in *Wooton Rivers,* but Holt had treated that as a special case and never said that the under-ten-pounds requirement of the statute was not jurisdictional.

The first case in which the "face of the record" rule was unambiguously applied to a statutory requirement was a summons case. In *The King v. Inhabitants of Woodsterton,*[52] two justices of peace ordered an overseer of the poor to make certain payments for poor relief. By the statute (9 George, c. 7) this was not to be done "until such Justice hath summoned two of the overseers of the poor to show cause why such relief should not be given." Mr. Wirley, of counsel, argued "he conceived the Words

52 2 Barnard. K.B. 207, 247 at 248 (1733).

of the Statute of 9 Geo. were penned so strong, that the Justices had not even a Jurisdiction" without a summons. But the court replied "they took it these were only Matters of Direction concerning the Proceeding of the Justices, and not concerning their Jurisdiction."

The effect of *Wooton Rivers* and *Woodsterton,* allowing the "face of the record" rule to be applied to some provisions of statute, was to invest the court with a great deal of discretion. Unless the justices chose to state the facts specially, their orders need comply with statute only in those factors which the court had labeled "jurisdictional." More often than not, moreover, the statute gave no guidance as to what factors were to be considered as "jurisdictional." Precedent and the obligation to do justice called for a scope of review which was much broader than that suggested by conceptual logic; fortunately, as was suggested in the introduction, the sense of justice usually won.

We have seen how, in the seventeenth century, two new legal remedies were developed from rather obscure origins and how each became in some measure a means by which a citizen could demand legality from his government. At the beginning the consciously held theory of mandamus was wholly a matter of "jurisdiction" and that of certiorari to quash was partly so; but for lack of theoretical clarity both remedies were in fact available for every issue of law. Somewhat paradoxically, mandamus became explicitly as well as practically available to enforce any legal right (for which no other remedy was available), while by the new eighteenth-century application of the "face of the record" rule the theoretical basis for certiorari became more and more "jurisdictional."

Yet the same theoretical vagueness which had allowed this development in the first place, plus an accumulation of precedents, kept certiorari available to review many rules of decision below, by means of various *ad hoc* extensions of the notion of jurisdiction. By this development King's Bench was invested with a great deal of power, since its decision to call a given question "jurisdictional" or otherwise was on the whole unfettered. The fact that on the whole so little injustice resulted in the cases from a doctrine so arbitrary as the "face of the record" rule speaks well for an independent judiciary; but this was accomplished only at a price of conscious or unconscious obfuscation. Perhaps this illustrates both the strength and the weakness of case law as a lawmaking process.

Appendix A

THE CONTROLMENT ROLLS

The Controlment Rolls of King's Bench are a separate series of rolls (K.B. 29) extending from the third year of Edward III (1329-30) to 1843. In physical appearance they are like the plea rolls or Coram Rege rolls, being made up of sheets of parchment, about nine by thirty inches, bound together at one end; but while a plea roll may have over 1000 membranes for a single term, a long controlment roll has perhaps 150-200 pages for a full year. They contain primarily writs original and judicial, with their returns, and other orders of the court including judgments, but not the pleadings. Giuseppi says[1] that they are concerned only or primarily with criminal cases, but it is my impression that writs in civil suits are also entered here, at least in the seventeenth century. For each term the entries are divided in three groups, called by Giuseppi "bag roll," "roll of entries," and "special writ roll." Except that most of the entries in the first group are very brief, it is not clear to me how the first and second groups are distinguished. The third, or "special writ roll," contains the writs which are here discussed, mandamus, certiorari, habeas corpus, and prohibition as well as error, quo warranto, and various others.

1 Montague S. Giuseppi, *A Guide to the Manuscripts Preserved in the Public Record Office* (London, 1923), pp. 226-227.

Within each part of the controlment rolls the entries are roughly chronological, as in a journal (except that the return to a writ is entered with the writ itself), in contrast to the plea rolls, where all the entries for a given case are made in one place. The early controlment rolls, according to Giuseppi, contain cross references to the plea rolls; but this was no longer done by the late sixteenth century.

Thus the controlment rolls are adequate only for a few purposes of research, but for these purposes they are very much more accessible and easier to use than the plea rolls. For the early history of mandamus they are probably the only source, as the first writs of mandamus were not entered on the plea rolls unless a return had been made.

Appendix B

WRITS OF RESTITUTION BEFORE JAMES BAGGE

1. *Thomas Tompson,* Controlment Roll no. 246, m. 125.

Cambridge, ss. The king, etc., to the mayor, bailiffs, and burgesses of our borough of Cambridge in the said county, and all of them, greetings. It has been shown to us on the part of Thomas Tompson, one of the burgesses of the said borough, that whereas in the said borough there are and for a long time past have been four bailiffs from among the burgesses of the said borough, exercising the office of bailiff for and during one whole year, which said bailiffs, after they have been duly elected and chosen and sworn to execute that office well and faithfully before the end of the said year, ought to be deposed or removed from that office by Us and Our Court and not by anyone else before the end of the said year, nor can or ought the said oath of each of them be dispensed or abrogated by anyone except by Us, Our heirs and successors, Whereas moreover all bailiffs of the said borough duly elected, chosen and sworn have had and enjoyed and have used to have and enjoy and each of them has had and enjoyed and has used to have and enjoy by reason of his execution of his said office diverse [*grandia,* perhaps "payments"] fees, pledges, fines, rents, tolls and other emoluments pertaining to his said office, and the present-day bailiffs of the said borough ought to have and enjoy such fees, pledges, fines, rents, tolls and other emoluments; And We have recently granted by Our letters patent sealed with the great seal of England, among other things, that the said borough should be a free borough and that the men of the said borough should be free burgesses and that they should have all their liberties and free customs belonging to the said borough in perpetuity, And that you the said mayor, bailiffs and burgesses of the same borough and also the burgesses of that borough whether legitimately incorporated before then or not, should henceforth forever, without any question or ambiguity to be thereafter made, be a body corporate and politic in deed and name, by the name of mayor, bailiffs and burgesses of the borough of Cambridge. And We have erected, made, ordered, constituted and given by the same Our letters patent to the same burgesses by the name of mayor, bailiffs, and burgesses of Cambridge, a body corporate and politic in act and name, really and in full, for Ourselves and Our heirs and successors. And that by that name they should have perpetual concession [succession]. And we have further granted and confirmed to you and your successors from Ourselves and all Our successors in any manner all such grants, both these and others like them, of free customs, liberties, privileges, franchises, immunities, quittances, exemptions, emoluments, lands, tenements, and hereditaments whatsoever, which you, and any of you now legitimately had, held, enjoyed and used or ought to have, hold or enjoy by the name of mayor, bailiffs and burgesses of the borough of Cambridge or by the name of bailiffs and burgesses of the borough of Cambridge or by any other name, or by any incorporation or body politic or other pretext of incorporation promised or given or granted to you or any of you or any of your predecessors by reason or pretext of any charters or letters patent by any of Our progenitors or ancestors however then made or confirmed or granted, or by pretext of any charters or letters patent by any of Our progenitors or ancestors however then made or confirmed or granted, or by pretext of any legitimate prescription, use or custom formerly had or used or by any other legal mode or title, even though the same or any of them has not formerly been used or has been abused or misused or discontinued, or even though the same or any of them was lost or forfeited, to have and hold and enjoy to yourselves and your successors as appears more fully by Our same letters patent which remain to you, And whereas moreover the said Thomas Tompson and one Richard Hull, Barnabas Claydon and Hugh Rose, being burgesses of the said borough, after the issuance of our said letters patent, namely at Michaelmas last past, were elected and chose as bailiffs of the said borough to serve in the said office for the whole year next following, and then and there the said corporal oath was offered to each of them to execute the said office well and faithfully, wherefore the same Thomas Tompson, Richard Hull, Barnabas Claydon and Hugh Rose and each of them ought to have and enjoy the said fees, pledges, fines, rents, tolls and other emoluments belonging to their said offices, as has been said,—You nevertheless, the mayor and burgesses of the said borough, thereafter, in the said borough, congregated together, excluding and leaving out the bailiffs of that borough, and there, by the sinister and malicious instigation and persuasion of you the now mayor of that borough and because of frivolous and private quarrels and controversies between you the said mayor and the said Thomas Tompson, Richard Hull and Barnabas Claydon, and excluding the said bailiffs who for the good government of the said borough ought to have been present at all of your meetings and votes, not having called them to this meeting at all and without their assent and consent, without notice to the same bailiffs and without Our command or the command of Our Court, did deprive, depose and remove the said Thomas Tompson from the office of one of the bailiffs of the said borough, or wholly illegitimately and without reasonable cause procured him to be deprived and removed. And because the said Thomas Tompson, according to his allegiance to Us and his said oath, wished thereafter to exercise and execute his said office, You nevertheless the said mayor caused the same Thomas to be arrested by your deputies as he was coming to Our Court of King's Bench at Westminster last Michaelmas term to talk with his counsel and attorneys to have their advice in a certain plea of debt sued in the same court by the same Thomas against one Christopher Hutchinson, on a demand of sixteen pounds and now pending undetermined, and detained him in Our prison called the Tolbooth in the said borough, in your custody, and you still detain him, Wherefore the said Thomas is the less able to exercise his said office as bailiff of the said borough as he ought and as he is bound to by his oath, nor can he pursue the said action in Our said court, as justice requires, And moreover you the said mayor and burgesses, excluding and leaving out the said bailiffs, have named another burgess of the said borough as one of the bailiffs of the said borough in the place of the said Thomas Tompson, and are illegitimately and without due form conspiring to have him elected, chosen and sworn, and have imposed or caused to be imposed other enormities and intolerable burdens on him the same Thomas in contempt of Us and to the damage, prejudice, scandal and pauperization of the said Thomas and in pernicious example and great derogation of the dignity of Our Crown. And the same Thomas has asked Us to provide him with an appropriate remedy, and We wishing that in this matter justice should be done to the said Thomas, and in order to preserve inviolate the liberties and privileges of Our said Court and of Our lieges who may sue any case in Our same Court without any indignity, vexation or hindrance, and not wishing that the liberties and ancient customs of the said borough should be violated or changed nor that any of Our lieges should be unduly burdened or disturbed by them, We order you and each of you, firmly enjoining you, that if the said Thomas Tompson is held in Our prison and under your custody for this reason and no other, then you and each of you shall allow the same Thomas to go at large, and you shall restore and cause to be restored the said Thomas Tompson without delay to his said office as one of the bailiffs of the said borough, along with everything pertaining to this office and which he lost for the aforesaid reason. And if you have elected or chosen anyone else in the place of the said Thomas, then you shall remove and cause to be removed that person thus newly elected from the said office, at your peril. Attested by J. Popham at Westminster, 30 January, in the third year of the King's reign in England, Ireland and France and in Scotland the thirty-ninth.

2. *Edward Farndon,* Controlment Roll no. 249, m. 16.

The King, etc. to the mayor, aldermen and sheriffs of London, and each of them, greeting. Whereas We, recently learning by the grave complaint of Edward Farndon, citizen and mercer of London in our court of King's Bench, that the same Edward Farndon had long been detained and incarcerated by your order in our gaol of Newgate, London, in close custody of the warden of the said gaol, by your order, without reasonable cause and contrary to the law and custom of our realm of England, to the grave damage and loss of the same Edward, We recently ordered you and the said warden of our gaol of Newgate by our writ to have the body of the same Edward, detained in the said gaol in the custody of the said warden, as it is said, with the date and cause of his imprisonment, before Our court at Westminster on the Monday next after the octave of Hillary term then next following, to submit and receive what Our said court should then and there decide in this matter, And you on that day informed and made return to Us that before the arrival of the same Our writ thus directed to you, as aforesaid, namely at the Session for delivering our gaol of Newgate held for the city of London at the Justice hall in the owld Baylye in the parish of St. Sepulchre in the suburbs of London, on the nineteenth of January in the fifth year of our reign in England, France and Ireland and in Scotland the forty-first, before you the said mayor and your then colleagues, our Justices assigned to deliver Our said gaol of the prisoners therein, the said Edward Farndon was solemnly exacted and he then and there appeared personally. And because then and there it fully appeared to the said court (of the said Session) by the testimony of various of Our trustworthy lieges that the same Edward Farndon then and long before then was a person of exceedingly bad name and fame and disgraceful conversation, a common barrator and a great disturber of the peace, a turbulent, litigious, assiduous and public sower of discords and wrangling among his neighbors and other Our lieges living and inhabiting in the said city, And that the same Edward Farndon, maliciously and scandalously intriguing, and intending to bring odium, contempt and ill-fame on one William Bedwell, Rector of the parish church of St. Ethelburga in the said London, being a pious, religious, and honorable man and a professor of sacred theology, insulted the same William Bedwell with many infamous scandals and curses, And procured one Thomas Andrews, being a person of exceedingly bad name and fame and disgraceful conversation, to write publish and divulge certain libels containing divers infamous and vicious abuse and false and scandalous matter against the said William Bedwell and a certain Thomas Thomlynson, a citizen and grocer of the said London, being an honorable man and a near neighbor of the said Edward Farndon, living in the said city, For which certain reasons and for many other misdeeds of the said Edward Farndon, both by word and deed, charged and brought forward in the said court before the said Justices, the same Edward Farndon was then and there committed by the said court to the said gaol of Newgate, to remain there until he should find sufficient [security] for his good behavior from then on toward Us and all Our people, And that this was the reason for the taking and detention of the said Edward Farndon in the said prison, You however had the body of the said Edward Farndon ready before Us then and there, as you had been ordered by Our same writ,—as appears to Us of record by that writ and your return made thereunto, which is kept attached to the record. And because it sufficiently appeared to Our court of King's Bench then and there that the said Edward Farndon before his said committal to Our said gaol of Newgate by Our said Justices on the aforesaid occasion in the said manner, came into Our court of King's Bench three weeks after Trinity in the fifth year of Our reign in England and France and in Scotland the fortieth, and then and there found Us sufficient security of the peace and for his good behavior toward Us and all Our people until the day after Trinity then next following, And that during the said term he would behave himself well toward Us and all Our people, namely that in the meantime he would not do nor cause to be done directly or indirectly any damage or bodily injury by means of insults or in any other way which could cause the peace to be broken or disturbed in any way, as plainly appears by the record in Our court of King's Bench; and that your return then and there made in the manner aforesaid was wholly defective, frivolous and uncertain, and the said causes so certified by you for the arrest and detention of the same Edward are invalid and insufficient in law to coerce or constrain the said Edward to find any other or further security of the peace or good behavior toward Us and all Our people during the said term. Therefore it was then and there considered by the same court that the said Edward should be discharged of finding any further security of the peace or good behavior and should be set at large, as in Our court of King's Bench plainly appears by the record. And now it is shown to us by the said Edward in Our court of King's Bench, deeply complaining, that although the same

Edward many years ago was duly and legitimately admitted to the liberties and freedom of the said city And has used to have and enjoy such liberties and franchises in the said city as the other citizens of the same estate and condition of the said Edward have used to have and enjoy and at present have and enjoy—Nevertheless, for the reasons stated in your said return certified as above, and because of the prosecution by the said Edward of a certain writ of Supersedeas on his said security of the peace and of good behavior, found in the King's Bench, (before the aforesaid Session of gaol delivery of Our said gaol of Newgate above specified) prosecuted, at another time and directed and delivered to you, you have entirely excluded the said Edward from his liberties and freedoms in the said city and have decreed that he shall lose them completely, and have caused the doors and windows of his shop and dwelling-house in the said city to be shut up and guarded, in which the said Edward, like the other citizens of the said city, was and is accustomed to show divers goods and merchandise for sale and distribution, and have imposed and caused to be imposed many other heavy and intolerable burdens on him. Whereby the same Edward cannot enjoy his liberties and franchises for the maintenance and sustenance of the said Edward and his family as he ought, according to the law and custom of Our realm of England and as our other lieges profit by them, in contempt of Us and to the grave damage and loss of the said Edward, and in pernicious example if this is permitted in the future, wherefore the same Edward has begged Us to give him Our aid and remedy. And We, hearing the prayer and complaint of the said Edward favorably and graciously, and not wishing that Our subjects should be burdened, vexed or hindered in any way because they seek justice in our court of King's Bench (as all Our lieges may do freely and with impunity) Not wishing, however, that your rights in this matter should be injured in any way, on the complaint of the said Edward, by consideration of Our said court We recently ordered that unless you should show sufficient cause to the contrary in Our said court on the Tuesday five weeks after Easter then next following, that then Our writ should issue from Our court directed to you to restore the said Edward to his former liberties and franchises in the said city, And you on that day or since have not at all cared to show Us any cause to the contrary but have totally neglected it. Therefore We order you, and all of you, firmly enjoining, both for the sake of complete justice and in execution of the order of Our said court, that if you or any of you have caused any doors or windows of the said shop or dwelling-house of the same Edward to be closed, or if you or any of you have caused the said Edward to be excluded from the liberties and franchises of the said city,—that you and each of you cause them to be opened without delay, and restore the said Edward to his former liberties and franchises in the said city without delay, not molesting or burdening the said Edward in any way on this account. And if you or any of you have done anything to the contrary, then you and each of you shall cause it to be relaxed and put right, at your peril. Attested by Thomas Flemynge at Westminster, on the third of May in the fifth year of our reign in England, France and Ireland, and in Scotland the forty-first. And in the following term an alias writ of restitution with a pain of forty pounds. And thereafter, in the following Michaelmas term a pluries writ of restitution with a pain of one hundred pounds returnable on the day after *All Souls.*

3. *Thomas Robinson*, Controlment Roll no. 249, m. 101.

Hertford, ss. The king, etc., to the mayor, bailiffs and burgesses of Our town of St. Albans in the county of Hertford and all of them, greetings. It has been shown to Us by Thomas Robinson, one of the common council of Our said vill that in that town there are and for a long time past have been a mayor, bailiffs and burgesses and twenty-four men of the common council, being officers duly elected and chosen for the better government of Our said town of St. Albans in the county of Hertford aforesaid, And that the twenty-four of the common council are duly sworn to execute their offices and for the execution of the same have had and enjoyed and have used to have and enjoy and each of them has had and enjoyed and has used to have and enjoy by reason of the execution of the said office various [*grandia,* perhaps "payments"] fees, fines, rents, and other emoluments pertaining to the said office and ought to have such fees, pledges, fines, rents, tolls and other emoluments and privileges. Now recently it has been further shown to Us by the said Thomas Robinson, grievously complaining in Our Court of King's Bench, that although the same Thomas has been duly and legitimately admitted to the society of the said twenty-four of the common council for many years long past, and to their liberties and franchises, and has used to have and enjoy the same liberties, privileges, franchises and emoluments in the said town, as the others of the said common council of the rank and condition of the same Thomas are used to have and enjoy and now have and enjoy in the same town,—You nevertheless the said mayor with the said bailiffs and burgesses, by the pretext of various misdeeds by him [three words illegible] without any reasonable cause certified to Us or Our Court have totally excluded the same Thomas Robinson from the liberties and franchises of the same town and have decreed that he shall lose them altogether. And you have imposed and caused to be imposed many other enormities and intolerable burdens upon him, Whereby the same Thomas is unable to enjoy his liberties, franchises and privileges for the maintenance and sustenance of himself and his family according to the law and custom of Our realm of England and as Our other lieges enjoy, as he ought, to the very grave damage of the said Thomas and in pernicious example in such cases if this should be allowed [one word illegible] Whereas the same Thomas has asked Us to give him appropriate aid and remedy in this matter, We, having heard the supplication and complaint of the said Thomas Robinson favorably and generously, not wishing that Our subjects should be vexed or burdened or hindered in any way because they seek justice in Our Court of King's Bench as all our lieges may do freely and with impunity, Wishing moreover that you in this matter should [not] be injured, on the complaint of the said Thomas Robinson, by consideration of Our said Court We ordered recently that unless you should show sufficient cause to the contrary on the Friday after Michaelmas then next following, there should issue from Our said Court Our writ directed to you to restore the said Thomas Robinson to his former liberties and privileges in the said town. And you have not cared on that day or since to show any cause to the contrary to Us or Our said Court of King's Bench but have wholly neglected to do so—We therefore strictly order you and all of you, both in fulfillment of justice and in execution of the aforesaid order and judgment of Our Court, firmly enjoining you, that if you have deposed and excluded the same Thomas Robinson from the liberties, franchises and privileges or from the society of the said twenty-four of the common council [two words illegible] or any one of you has caused him to be deposed or excluded, that without delay you restore the said Thomas Robinson to his former liberties, franchises and privileges and to the society of the aforesaid twenty-four of the common council of the said town, not molesting nor burdening the said Thomas in any way on this account, And if you or any of you have done anything to the contrary before this, then you and each of you shall release the same Thomas and make amends to him. And report to us how this Our order has been executed in the octave after Hillary wherever We may then be in England, And have there this writ. Tested by T. Flemynge at Westminster on the 22d day of November in the sixth year of the King's reign in England, France and Ireland and in Scotland the forty-second.

4. *William Broxholme,* Controlment Roll no. 254, m. 78.

The King etc. to the mayor, sheriff and commons of Our city of Lincoln, greetings. Whereas William Broxholme, knight, and Robert Townson, citizens of the said city, have recently shown to Us in Our court of King's Bench, grievously complaining, that although the same William and Robert were duly and legitimately admitted to the liberties and franchises of the city of Lincoln aforesaid many years ago, and have used to have and enjoy such liberties and franchises in the said city as other citizens of the estate and condition of the same William and Robert of the same city, have used to have and enjoy and now have and enjoy, You nevertheless the said mayor, sheriff and commons of the said city of Lincoln without any reasonable cause did wholly exclude the same William and Robert, and both of them, from their liberties and franchises in the said city and decreed that they should wholly lose them, and imposed and caused to be imposed upon them many other enormities and intolerable burdens, whereby the same William and Robert are unable to enjoy their liberties and franchises for the maintenance and sustenance of the same William and Robert and their families, as they ought, according to the law and custom of Our realm of England and as Our other lieges [one word illegible] enjoy them, in contempt of Us and to the no slight damage of the same William and Robert, and in pernicious example in this respect if it should be allowed in the future, We therefore wishing that due and prompt justice should be done to the said William and Robert in this matter, as is just, We order you, and all of you, firmly enjoining you, that immediately on the reception of this writ you restore or cause to be restored the said William Broxholme and Robert Townson and both of them to their former liberties and franchises of the said city, without delay, lest complaint come to Us of your default. And report to Us how this Our writ has been executed in the octave of Hillary wherever We may then be in England, returning this Our writ to Us then. Tested by T. Flemynge at Westminster, 20 November in the tenth year of the King's reign in England, France and Ireland, and in Scotland the forty-sixth.

5. *Richard Anable,* "in the time of Henry 6," printed 3 Dyer 333.

The King to the Mayor of the city of London, greeting. Whereas Richard Anable of London, pewterer, according to the laws and customs of Our realm of England, used and approved in Our times and those of Our ancestors, Kings of England hitherto, for all the liege subjects of Us and of Our aforesaid ancestors hath impleaded Thomas Fawconer of London, mercer, late escheator of our city aforesaid, of certain trespasses in Our Court of King's Bench by Our writ in that writ specified, committed against the said Richard as is said, yet on behalf of the aforesaid Richard, in Our court aforesaid before us, we have received grievous complaint, containing, that although the said Richard from long time back hath been admitted to the liberties and franchises of the city aforesaid, and has been used to have and enjoy such liberties and franchises within the said city as other fellow-citizens of his estate and condition in the said city have been accustomed to have and enjoy, as one of the fellow-citizens of the same city, from the time when he was admitted until he moved and prosecuted his plaint aforesaid for the trespass aforesaid against the aforesaid Thomas, in our court before us,—You by reason of the moving of the aforesaid plaint against the aforesaid Thomas, and the prosecution thereof elsewhere than before you within our city aforesaid, do intend to cause the said Richard to lose his liberties within our city aforesaid, and have caused the doors and windows of the dwelling-house of the said Richard, within the same city, to be shut and bolted, and have imposed and caused to be imposed upon him many other burdens not to be borne, whereby the said Richard is the less able to obtain justice in his said plaint of the trespass aforesaid in our said Court before us freely as our liege subject may do, in contempt of Us and to the great damage of the said Richard, and to the evil example in that behalf, and great derogation of Our royal crown and dignity, chiefly since Our Royal Prerogative which we and our ancestors have of right used, appertaineth to Our royal dignity as a right of Our crown annexed to Our person, that every liege man of Ours who will prosecute his right there should there freely obtain it without any scorn, vexation, grievance or impediment on that occasion, in any way, imposed upon him by anyone: We therefore command you, firmly enjoining, that if ye have caused to be shut up any doors or windows of the dwelling house of the said Richard for that reason, ye do cause them without delay to be opened . . .

Appendix C

CERTIORARI AND KINDRED WRITS

1. *Recordari, Registrum Omnium Brevium* (London, 1553), fo. 15.

Rex, etc. Precipimus tibi quod si A. fecerit te securum in pleno comitatu tuo recordari facias loquelam que est in eodem comitatu per breve nostrum de recto, inter A. petentem et B. tenentem de uno messuagio cum pertinenciis in C. unde idem A. queritur falsum sibi factum iudicium in eodem comitatu. Et recordum illud habeas coram justiciariis nostris apud Westmonasterium tali die, sub sigillo tuo et quattuor legalium militum eiusdem comitatus ex illis qui recordo illi interfuerunt. Et partibus eundem diem prefigas, quod tunc sint ibi in loquela illa prout justum fuerit processuri. Et habeas ibi nomina predictorum quatuor militum, et hoc breve.

The king, etc. We order you that, if A gives you security, you shall cause to be recorded in your full county court the plea which is in the same county court by Our writ of right, between A, demandant, and B, tenant, concerning a house with its appurtenances in C., because the same A complains that a false judgment was made against him in the same county court. And have that record before Our justices at Westminster on such a day, under your seal and the seals of four lawful knights of the same county court who were present when the said record was made. And warn the parties of the same day, so that they shall be there to proceed in the same plea as shall be just. And have there the names of the aforesaid four knights, and this writ.

2. *Accedas ad curiam, Reg. Brevium,* fo. 15a.

Rex, etc. vicecomiti. Si A. fecerit te securum tunc assumptis tecum quatuor discretis et legalibus militibus de comitatu tuo, in propria persona tua accedas ad curiam B. de C. et in plena curia illa recordari facias loquelam quae fuit in eadem curia . . . unde idem A. queritur falsum sibi factum fuisse iudicium in eadem curia. Et recordum illud habeas coram justiciariis nostris . . . sub sigillo tuo et sigillis quatuor legalium hominum eiusdem curiae ex illis qui recordo illi interfuerunt.

The king, etc., to the sheriff. If A gives you security, then taking with you four discreet and lawful knights of your county court, go personally to the court of B and in full court there cause to be recorded the plea which was in the same court . . . because the same A complains that a false judgment was made against him in the same court. And have that record before Our justices . . . under your seal and the seals of four lawful men of the same court who were present when that record was made.

3. *Certiorari* (varies a great deal, but this is the classic form).

Rex, etc. salutem. Quia certis de causis certiorari velimus super recordo et processu cuiusdam loquele . . . tibi precepimus quod recordum et processum predicta cum omnibus ea tangentibus nobis sub sigillo tuo distincte et aperte mittatis, et hoc breve, ita quod ea habeamus tali die ubicunque tunc fuerimus in Anglia, ut inspectis recordo et processu predictis ulterius inde fieri faciamus quod de jure et secundum legem et consuetudinem regni nostri Anglie fuerit faciendum.

The king, etc., greetings. Because We wish to be informed

for certain reasons about the record and process of a certain plea . . . we order you to send the aforesaid record and process with everything touching thereon to Us under your seal, distinctly and openly, and send this writ, so that We may have it on such a day wherever We may then be in England, so that having inspected the said record and process We may cause such further action to be taken as by right and according to the law and custom of Our realm of England ought to be taken.

4. Error, *Reg. Brevium*, fo. 16-17.

Rex justitiariis suis salutem. Quia in recordo et processu, ac etiam in redditione judicii loquele que fuit coram vobis . . . inter A. & B. de . . . error intervenit manifestus ad grave dampnum ipsius B., sicut ex querela sua accepimus: nos errorem si quis fuerit modo debito corrigi et eidem B. plenam et celerem justitiam fieri volens in hac parte: vobis mandamus quod si iudicium inde redditum sit, tunc recordum et processum loquele predicte cum omnibus ea tangentibus nobis sub sigillo vestro distincte et aperte mittatis, et hoc breve, ita quod ea habeamus . . .

The king to his justices, greetings. Because manifest error has occurred in the record and process, and also in the judgment rendered, in a plea which was before you . . . between A and B concerning . . . , to the grave damage of the said B, as we have learned from his complaint: We, wishing to correct the error, if there is any, in due manner, and wishing to do the same B full and speedy justice in this matter: We order you, if judgment therein has been rendered, to send the record and process with everything touching upon them, distinctly and openly, under your seal, with this writ, so that We may have it . . .

5. *R. v. Justices of Marlborough*, Controlment Roll no. 283, m. 125 (Mich., 11 Car., 1635).

Rex mandavit custodibus pacis suis . . . Volentes certis de

causis quendam ordinem ad generalem sessionem pacis nostre et visum franci plegii pro burgo predicto in Guildhallam ibidem tentam [6 Oct., 10 Car.] concernentes pistores coram vobis factum ut est dictum coram nobis per vobis mitti, vobis mandamus quod ordinem predictum cum omnibus ea tangentibus nobis sub sigillo tuo distincte et aperte mittatis . . . Teste T. Richardson, 20 Oct., 10 Car.

The king ordered his guardians of the peace . . . Wishing for certain reasons that a certain order made, it is said, at Our general sessions of the peace and view of frankpledge for the said borough in its Guildhall concerning bakers, should be sent before Us by you, We command you to send Us the said order with everything touching upon them, distinctly and openly under your seal . . .

Return to this writ: Forasmuch as there has been of late a new market house erected in the high street of the said borough to the great cost of the chamber which house so erected was specially intended to be for the placing selling and weighing of the wool butter and cheese that should from time to time be brought on the fair days and market days unto the said town to be sold & yet the common bakers of the said town since the erection of the said new house do on the market days place their standings there and thereby do annoy the market & although they have been heretofore commanded by the late mayor to forbear to place their standings in the said market house yet were licensed and directed to set their standings in the open street before Francis Dodson's house in a convenient place there but the said bakers have hitherto obstinately refused to do, it is therefore now ordered that if any of the said bakers or any other person shall at any time hereafter presume to place any stalls or standing in any part of the said market house without special license of the mayor & justices of the peace of this borough for the time being that then the said parties so presuming to place any stall or stand in the said market house shall find sureties for his or their good behavior & to appear at the next sessions of the peace to answer to his or their contempt.

Witnessed 27 Oct., anno supradicto.

This entry is followed on m. 126 by certiorari to the same justices for recognizances made by several named bakers, and by five such recognizances. Three of the latter are dated 11 October; two, 13 October.

Appendix D

COMMINS VERS SIR WILLIAM MASSUM

K.B., Easter 1642; Harvard Law School MS (Turner) 113, p. 170.

The case was thus: The father, lessee for years, covenants to sustain all charges to be imposed by the Commissioners of Sewers, for the defence or maintenance of the walls pertaining to his land. The Commissioners to prevent surrounding, decree the tenant (namely, the son and executor of the father, now dead) to build a new wall, next to the sea; he refuses. By consent of the Commissioners and the tenant, this was agreed to be the case, and certiorari was prayed in the King's Bench, on which, without any special verdict or demurrer, being a case in English, the Judges concluded, as follows:

Mallett Justice. Before 23 Henry VIII, c. 5 all pleadings before the Commissioners of Sewers were in Latin, but this case at bar is in English: the Commissioners *ex antiquo* were called *Justiciarii ad wallias et fossata supervidenda.* By the statute *supra* their Commission is in English and all their proceedings entered in English. They have legislative power to make laws and ordinances which are returnable in Chancery, and therefore, I conceive, not questionable here, neither by writ of error nor by any other means, but only in Parliament; and when their orders have the royal assent they are like acts of

Parliament: In London the Mayor's Court has a Chancery power, but if a case depending there should be removed here by certiorari, I conceive that we would have no power to intermeddle with it, for our power and Commission is legal only. Thus in the case at bar, the proceedings are in an equitable Chancery way, in such a course that this Court has no Cognizance, and inasmuch as the case and decree are in English I do not wish to deliver any opinion in the case. I admit that before 23 [Henry 8] when the Commission etc. were in Latin, there are many precedents of Judgments and decrees reversed in this Court, but since then none. And therefore I shall not speak.

Heath Justice. It seems to me that the Court has Jurisdiction of the case: I agree that before the statute of 23 Henry VIII the proceedings of the Commissioners of Sewers were in other form than now; but as the case at bar appears, the Certiorari is well granted and the case proper for our examination: No ordinary Judges in the Realm have this power, but this Court is *Coram Rege ipso*, and notwithstanding the act leaves the proceedings to the discretion of the Commissioners, nevertheless that discretion is examinable and controllable in this Court.

Admitting that the Commissioners of Sewers have done anything without or against their Commission, without doubt this is reformable and examinable here: But as for courts of Equity, as for the Marches of Wales and the like, this Court cannot take notice whether their decrees are just or not: We are to examine only *their Jurisdiction of the case, not their Justice*: They themselves shall answer for that, as we for the law: Let us put the case that A bargains and sells land to B and C gives collateral security to B; and the Commissioners make a decree against C, this is against law, and therefore reformable by us; but equitable cases are nothing to us.

In the case at bar they were punctual in their return: the Commission is [cited] *in hac verba*, the trial by Jury and the names of the Jury likewise, and it appears that they were twelve and this was necessary, for *per sacramentum juratorum* would have been bad, but *12 juratorum* would have been good. The case was agreed by both parties, and by the Commissioners also, and it was as above: It is clear that the lessee for years can be charged by the Commissioners, and we cannot remedy it: 5 Rep., Jeffryes case, lessee for years is chargeable for the repair of the church in his parish, even though he does not live there but only farms some land. Thus the Commissioners have power in their discretion to tax owners, or occupiers, by the statute. Commins in the case at bar was the tenant, and executor to his father who made the covenant, and the 1. commissioners imposed the tax on him alone and not on his lessor: as to this, I say that the covenant of necessity shall bind the tenant 2. and if the decree is unjust there is remedy in the Chancery. The Commissioners may well take notice of the Covenant of the lessee: inasmuch as they are Chancery judges and have cognizance of mixed cases, whereas we [have cognizance] only of law; and the consent of the tenant in this case was the ground of the decree. 3. But it was objected that the father was the occupier of the land when the charge was imposed, and since then the estate has come to his executor, and it does not appear that he had assets: etc. As to this, the case was agreed before the death of the tenant; but the executor being summoned before the Commissioners did not deny that there were assets, and therefore it will be presumed, and therefore the decree is good. If an action be brought in this Court against an Executor, and he pleads to the action and does not speak of assets, if the cause then proceeds, an averment that he has no assets will not delay Judgment; and if Judgment be given here, it will not be reversed in the Exchequer Chamber because the executor has no assets. I conclude that this court has jurisdiction of the decree of the Commissioners if it be illegal. But in the case at bar there is no injustice, and if the party conceive himself oppressed, he should repair to the Chancery to have more equity.

Bramston Chief Justice. If I had known of the case, I would not have granted the Certiorare, but it being granted, we must decide the case as it is: When a case of this nature is before us by Certiorare, even though there be good cause for allowing the proceedings before this, we cannot send back the cause; and if not, how shall the tax be levied? If it were merely a fine on the tenant, we could estreat it into the Exchequer, but not a tax: Therefore the parties were bound, by recognizance, not by coercion of the Court but voluntarily, that if the decree should be affirmed by the Court the money would be paid, and this tolls the mischief. As to the case: the lessee covenants to sustain all charges to be imposed for the maintenance of the walls appertaining to the land: The Commissioners decree a new wall adjoining the land, and the question is whether the Covenant extends to that. Every covenant is to be taken most strongly against the covenantor, and is to be construed so that it may be valid, and according to the intent of the parties: but if it is not construed as extending to his new wall it will be held void, for there is no other wall, but this one alone pertains to or is next to the land. In [Y.B.] 28 H. VIII is is said Contracts are like private laws, and against one's own act no averment [shall be heard]. But an objection was made at the bar to the Jurisdiction of the Commissioners, in that their power is solely limited to owners and occupiers and the case at bar is of a contract, which is a thing collateral to the land: As to this there are many cases in their power and discretion which are not named; as if one be bound by prescription, Custom, tenure, to repair the banks etc., the Commissioners may spare the owners and occupiers and impose the tax on those who are so bound: so also in case of a Covenant: 10 Rep., Keighley's Case. I grant that if a stranger covenants to save the tenant harmless the Commissioners have nothing to do with him: but it is otherwise if the lessee is the Covenantor. In the case at bar it is true that the party against whom the decree was made is an executor, but he is also an assignee of the land; and it will be intended that he has assets, inasmuch as the Contrary does not appear. It was moved at the Bar that in that case Massam should have recompense above his money. For to save the level from surrounding he expended his own money: it was agreed by the Commissioners, and I conceive it legal, that they would decree enough for the main works, and payment to the expenditor also: If one who is taxed refuses to pay and another deposits for him, it is quite reasonable that the Commissioners should consider the satisfaction of the latter: for otherwise for the misdemeanors of one or two inhabitants the whole level will be surrounded before the collection can be made. F.N.B. 113, 114. The Commissioners of Sewers are Justices; they have a Court; the new commissioners have power to take notice of and retain pending proceedings, as well as to entertain new [proceedings.] It was also objected at the bar that here Sir Will Massum had obtained the decree against one who is not interested in the original suit and therefore he is without remedy: as to this observe that in every case where the party is privy he must have a writ of error or a Certiorare: but if he is otherwise concerned in point of interest he must falsify [traverse] the Judgment. In the case at bar I affirm the decree.

Appendix E

THE POWTE'S COMPLAINT: A "LIBELLOUS SONG" ON THE DRAINING OF THE GREAT LEVEL

Come, Brethren of the water, and let us all assemble,
To treat upon this matter, which makes us quake and tremble,
For we shall rue it, if't be true, that Fens be undertaken,
And where we feed in Fen and Reed, they'll feed both Beef and Bacon.

They'll sow both beans and oats, where never man yet thought it,
Where men did row in boats, ere undertakers bought it:
But Ceres, thou behold us now, let wild oats be their venture,
Oh, let the frogs and miry bogs destroy where they do enter.

Behold the great design, which they do now determine,
Will make our bodies pine, a prey to crows and vermine:
For they do mean all Fens to drain, and waters overmaster
All will be dry, and we must die, 'cause Essex calves want pasture.

Away with boats and rudder, farewell both boots and skatches,

No need of one nor th'other, men now make better matches;
Stilt-makers all and tanners shall complain of this disaster;
For they will make each muddy lake for Essex calves a pasture . . .

Wherefore let us intreat our ancient water nurses
To show their power so great as t'help to drain their purses;
And send us good old Captain Flood to lead us out to battle,
Then two-penny Jack, with skales on's back, will drive out all the cattle . . .

Great Neptune (God of seas), this work must needs provoke thee
They mean thee to disease [disseise] and with Fen water choak thee;
But with thy mace, do thou deface, and quite confound this matter;
And send thy sands, to make dry lands, when they shall want fresh water.

And eke we pray thee, Moon, that thou wilt be propitious,
To see that nought be done, to prosper the malicious;
Though summer's heat hath wrought a feat, whereby themselves they flatter,
Yet be so good as send a flood, lest Essex calves want water.

—William Dugdale, *History of Imbanking and Draining of Divers Fens and Marshes* (London, 1772), pp. 391-392.

BIBLIOGRAPHY

PRIMARY SOURCES

The most important primary sources for legal developments are the reports of cases adjudged in the central courts at Westminster. Lists of the reports for this period will be found in volumes V and VI of Holdsworth, *History of English Law*. Other primary sources consulted were:

Acts of the Privy Council, 1570-1630. London, 1893-1960.

Calendar of Close Rolls, 1251-1272. London, 1922-1938.

Flower, Cyril, *Public Works in Mediaeval Law*. Selden Society vol. 32, 40, London, 1915 and 1923.

Hertfordshire County Records. Hertford, 1928.

Lincoln Corporation Register, in Historical Manuscripts Commission, Fourteenth Report, Appendix, part 8, London, 1895.

Leicester, Records of the Borough of, M. Bateson, ed. Oxford, 1880.

London County Council, *Court Minutes of the Surrey and Kent Sewers Commission*. London, 1909.

Nottingham, Records of the Borough of. Nottingham, 1889.

Oxford, Selections from the Records of the City of, W. H. Turner, ed. Oxford, 1880.

Reading, Records of the Borough of, J. M. Guilding, ed. London, 1895.

Registrum Omnium Brevium. References to 1553 edition, London, Richard Tottell.

Sayles, G. O., ed., *Select Cases in the Court of King's Bench under Edward I*. Selden Society, vols. 55, 57, 58, London, 1936-1939.

Somerset Quarter Sessions Records. London, 1907.

Thesaurus Brevium. 2nd ed., London, W. Rawlins and others, 1687.

Warwick County Records. Warwick, 1935.

Yorkshire Archaeological Society, *West Riding Quarter Sessions Records.* Record Series, v. 54, Leeds, 1915.

Unpublished records and manuscripts:

H. M. Public Record Office, London:

Controlment Rolls, Court of King's Bench, 1585-1642.

Plea Rolls, King's Bench, 1605-1607.

Harvard Law School:

L MS 2074.

MS 52.

MS (Turner) 113.

CONTEMPORARY SECONDARY SOURCES

Blackstone, Sir William, *Commentaries on the Laws of England.*

Brooke, Sir Robert, *La Graunde Abridgement.* London, Richard Tottell, 1586.

Callis, Robert, *Reading upon the Statute of Sewers* (given at Gray's Inn, 1622). Harvard Law School L MS 1053, signed *Per me Robertum Callis Lectorem;* and London, William Leak, 1647.

Coke, Sir Edward, *The Second Part of the Institutes of the Lawes of England.* London, M. Flesher and R. Young, 1642.

—— *The Fourth Part of the Institutes of the Lawes of England.* London, M. Flesher, 1648.

Crompton, R., *L'Authorite et Jurisdiction des Courts de la Roygne.*

Dalton, Michael, *The Countrey Justice,* London, Society of Stationers, 1618.

Dugdale, William, *History of Imbanking and Draining of Divers Fens and Marshes . . . ,* second edition, London, W. Bowyer and J. Nichols, 1772.

[Fitzherbert, Sir Anthony], *Diversite de Courts et lour jurisdictions et alia necessaria et utilia.*

Fitzherbert, Sir Anthony, *Novel Natura Brevium.*

Hale, Sir Matthew, *Pleas of the Crown.*

Kitchin, John, *Le Court Leete et Court Baron.* London, Company of Stationers, 1623.

Lambard, William, *Eirenarcha, or the Office of a Justice of the Peace.* London, Company of Stationers, 1610.

—— *The Dueties of Constables.* London, Thomas Wight and Bonham Norton, 1599.

Rolle, Sir Henry, *Un Abridgement des Plusieurs Cases et Resolutions del Common Ley*. London, A. Crooke and others, 1668.

Style, William, *Regestum Practicale, or the Practical Register*. London, by A. M. for Charles Adams, 1657.

Viner, Charles, *A General Abridgement of Law and Equity* . . . 2nd ed., London, Robinson and others, 1791.

MODERN WORKS

Chafee, Zechariah, Jr., *Some Problems in Equity*. Ann Arbor, Mich., 1950.

Cohen, Maxwell, "*Some Considerations on the Origins of Habeas Corpus.*" 16 Canadian Bar Review 92 (1938).

——— "*Habeas Corpus cum Causa — The Emergence of the Modern Writ.*" 18 Canadian Bar Review 10 (1940).

Cunnington, B. Howard, *Some Annals of the Borough of Devizes*. Devizes, 1925.

Giuseppi, Montague S., *A Guide to the Manuscripts Preserved in the Public Record Office*. London, 1923.

Griffith, J. A. G. and Street, H., *Principles of Administrative Law*. London, 1952.

Holdsworth, W. E., *History of English Law*. 6th ed., London, 1938.

Maine, Sir Henry, *Early Law and Custom*. London, 1883.

Milsom, S. F. C., "*The Origins and Early History of Judicial Review in England.*" Unpublished diss., University of Cambridge, 1957.

Putnam, Bertha, *Proceedings before the Justices of Peace in the Fourteenth and Fifteenth Centuries*. Ames Foundation, London, 1938.

Thorne, S. E., *Sir Edward Coke, 1552-1952*. London, 1957.

CASES CITED

STATUTES CITED

INDEX

For statutes and decided cases, see the separate tables of statutes cited and cases cited.

Bei Fragen zur Produktsicherheit wenden Sie sich bitte an:
If you have any questions regarding product safety,
please contact:

Walter de Gruyter GmbH
Genthiner Straße 13
10785 Berlin
productsafety@degruyterbrill.com